BEST BUSINESS PRACTICES

Keys to Success

By

Ralph Coker

Copyright 2023 by Ralph Coker

All Rights Reserved

All rights reserved. No part of this book may be used or reproduced in any manner whatsoever without the express written permission of the writer, except in the case of brief quotations embodied in critical essays and reviews.

For more information contact
Ralph Coker

Cover/Manuscript Formatting by William Mays

© 2023 Ralph Coker
All rights reserved.

Printed in the United States of America

ISBN 9798395926494

Non-Fiction: Business
Non-Fiction: Small Business

Dedication

I dedicate this book to my wife, Kathy. When I retired, she encouraged me to volunteer to provide free help and coaching to small business owners and managers, instead of sitting home bored out of my mind. That created another great adventure. She has been my computer "techie", political sensitivity monitor and editor. Without her help, I could not have written this book.

I appreciate the help of Tom Whitehurst, business editor of our local newspaper. He created the opportunity for me to write a weekly business advice column for 17 years and taught me newspaper writing techniques.

I appreciate my 600 plus clients who allowed me to share their challenges, successes and a few failures.

I appreciate the reporters of The Wall Street Journal who keep me informed with timely information about current business issues and trends.

PREFACE

My education is a Bachelor of Industrial Engineering degree from Georgia Tech. I spent my 45-year career in oil refining, starting as an engineer and rising to Operations Manager and refinery Plant Manager. As a plant manager, I learned that small local service businesses were more efficient, reliable, cost effective and had the best quality work. After retiring in 2001, I volunteered to provide free help and coaching to small business owners and managers. I worked with more than 600 clients and shared their challenges, successes, and a few failures. From them, I learned what works in business and more important, what does not work. This book contains those lessons learned. I hope the reader finds the book as satisfying to read as I did to write it.

Best wishes for your business success.

DISCLAIMER

The advice in this book is generic and may apply to all types of businesses; however, each business is unique with its own challenges, opportunities, and risks. Readers should evaluate the advice for themselves and determine whether it applies in their business and if so, how it applies.

Table of Contents

Chapter One
Keys to Business Success and Ownership   8

Chapter Two
Marketing and Selling   14

Chapter Three
Financial Planning and Management   62

Chapter Four
Business Management Skills   85

Chapter Five
Worker Productivity   123

Chapter Six
Starting a New Business   135

Chapter Seven
Hiring and Training   164

Chapter Eight
Other Good Advice   182

CHAPTER ONE

KEYS TO BUSINESS SUCCESS AND OWNERSHIP

SUMMARY

- Large success consists of many small tasks done well.

- It is the size of your heart that counts, not your brain or personality.

- Persistence and endurance always win over brilliance.

- As in sports, luck sometimes brings business success; however, you must be in the game, not safe on the sidelines.

CHAPTER 1

KEYS TO BUSINESS SUCCESS AND OWNERSHIP

1-1 What Are the Keys to Business Success?　　10
1-2 What Are the Keys to Small Business Success?　　12

1-1 Q. What are the keys to business Success?

We must learn 10 lessons to success in business. I'll use examples from business to illustrate how the 10 lessons apply. First, to succeed in business, diligently complete the little detail tasks. Large successes consist of many little tasks completed successfully.

Second, to succeed in business, find a team to help you. You need the help of friends, work colleagues, advisors, mentors, family members, your boss and sometimes the goodwill of strangers. None of us have the knowledge, skills and abilities to succeed alone in a very complex world.

Third, success in business depends on the size of your heart not the size of your brain or personality. You have to want success more than anything in the world and be willing to sacrifice through physical, mental and emotional hardships to reach it. Success is a marathon not a sprint. Persistence and endurance will always win over brilliance.

Fourth, to succeed in business and life, we have to learn that life is not always fair. Despite our most diligent efforts we fail sometimes for reasons that are not our fault. Others harm us and are not punished. We fail to get the job of our dreams or that promotion we deserve. We can't stop the world and get off. We have to keep moving forward.

Fifth, to succeed in business learn to survive failure and through failure to become stronger and better prepared to succeed next time. We all fail, it's just a question of how many times we fail. If the failure is our fault, we have to analyze why we failed and resolve not to repeat it. Failure is very painful to our egos. We have to learn to accept failure, forgive ourselves, get over it and move on with our lives. Above all don't become obsessed with fear of failure and not take on challenges.

Sixth, to succeed in business we have to take risks. Not foolish risks. Carefully calculated risks where the potential reward is always worth the potential consequences of failure. In my career I found that business success was about 50 percent chance, 40 percent knowledge, skill and dedication and 10 percent innovation meaning finding a better way to do things. However, you have to be in the game for chance to make you a winner. You can't be safe on the sidelines.

Seventh, to succeed in business you must have the courage to defend yourself from the sharks in this world that want to do you harm.

Eighth, to succeed in business you must be able to remain calm and perform your best under the worst conditions. That means when there's great uncertainty, confusion, distractions and fear. In business that could be a recession, key employee injury or death.

Ninth, to succeed in business you have to have hope. When that worst condition happens, you need your best brains, knowledge, skills and judgment but only hope will get you through it. Otherwise you will give up and fail. Tenth, to succeed in business never give up. I had a very successful manager reporting to me at one time who overcame every obstacle with such determination and persistence that he just ground the obstacles to dust. I too found persistence beat brilliance every time.

1-2 Q. What are the Keys to Small Business Success

A. There are many keys to small business success but five stand out from all the others. First, the owner must know how to produce the product or service the business provides to the customer. The business may have employees who produce the product or service, but the owner must know how to train and supervise the employees. Occasionally, I get a client who wants to start or buy a business that they know absolutely nothing about. That's likely to lead to certain failure. If the person doesn't know the business, they should work for someone else in that business and learn it.

Second, the owner needs good management skills including planning, delegating, organizing, coordinating, communication and follow up. Franchisors will accept prospective franchisees who don't know the business because they want to teach the franchisee their successful business model, however they insist the prospect have good management skills.

Third, the owner must know the basic business functions of marketing, sales, advertising, bookkeeping, financial management, insurance, taxes, accounts receivable and credit. It's difficult for one person to be skilled in all functions. Often an owner will have a partner, spouse or key employee who handles some of the duties, however the owner still needs to know all functions to make good business decisions.

Fourth, the business needs sufficient working capital in cash or credit to cover fluctuations in sales revenue, inventory cost and expenses. If the business is a start up, it should expect to have losses each month until sales revenue ramps up to reach breakeven where revenue is sufficient to cover cost of goods sold and expenses. The owner should estimate the number of months and working capital required to reach breakeven and add at least 20 percent to cover errors in estimating. An existing business needs working capital to cover seasonal fluctuations in sales revenue, large expense payments like insurance or business recessions. Some businesses operate without credit and pay current bills from current sales revenue and credit cards. That works when business is good. However, when the recession came, many of those failed because they couldn't get bank credit after the business was already in trouble.

Fifth, owners need to be good cash flow managers. Cash is king. A business can be profitable according to its profit and loss statement but still go bankrupt if it doesn't have cash or credit to pay bills when due. Each business should maintain a rolling projected cash flow chart projecting cash receipts and cash payments for each of the next 12 months. Update the chart at the end of each month. If the chart shows a cash shortage approaching, arrange for credit to cover the short fall.

The above keys to success apply to all businesses, however each industry has its own additional keys to success that apply to that industry.

CHAPTER TWO

MARKETING AND SELLING

SUMMARY

- Marketing is what you do to get potential customers in the door of your store or office or on your website and social media pages. Selling is what you do to make a sale after they are there.

- Marketing and selling are the essential life blood of a business. If the business owner or manager are unwilling to be the chief marketer and salesperson, find other employment.

- Each market is unique. If a product or service sells well in one market, that does not mean it will sell well in other markets.

- Business should strive to achieve two thirds of their customers as loyal, repeat customers. Two thirds of their new customers should come by referral form their loyal, repeat customers.

- Discount to make a profitable sale this time or in the future. Never discount at a loss.

CHAPTER TWO

MARKETING AND SELLING

2-1 Retail Sales Techniques	16
2-2 Direct Outside Sales Techniques	18
2-3 Online Marketing Opportunities	20
2-4 Customer for Freelance	22
2-5 Defense from Online Competition	24
2-6 Customer Referrals	26
2-7 Discounting as a Marketing Tool	28
2-8 Marketing Plan for Low-cost retail Items	30
2-9 Handling Customer complaints	32
2-10 Competing with Online Marketing	34
2-11 Keeping Customers Loyal	35
2-12 Repeat Customer Marketing	37
2-13 Data Driven Marketing	39
2-14 Determining if a Customer Will Buy	40
2-15 Getting and retaining customer for Service Business	42
2-16 Good Net Working Practices	44
2-17 Marketing New Products	46
2-18 Establishing Brand Name	48
2-19 Marketing to Millennials	50
2-20 New Consumer Product	52
2-21 Customer Self Service	54
2-22 Limiting Returns	56
2-23 Hiring A Sales-Person	58
2-24 What do my Customers Want?	60

2-1 Q. How can I increase sales for my retail business?

A. Your marketing plan gets the customer in the door and you may have a super marketing plan but if you can't make the sale your business will fail. Unfortunately, too many retail businesses don't prepare and train their sales staff to make the sale. Your sales staff must know everything about the product or service that the customer will want to know. Know as much about your customer's wants and needs as possible. Depending on the product, have take away brochures describing the product, its usefulness and operation. For certain products the customer expects inventory on hand to choose from and for immediate delivery. For other products order placement is customary. The sales area should be well lighted, freshly painted, clean and attractive especially at the entry for a good first impression. Arrange the merchandise for good visibility and convenience. Put impulse items near the cash register or front door.

When you greet the customer make them feel comfortable as if they were in your home. Try to encourage confidence in the store, the salesperson, and the product. The best listener is the best salesperson not the one who talks most. Listen to determine the customer's wants and needs and what they value most: low price-good quality- good service after the sale-lots of choices-convenience. Listen first and then respond accordingly.

Look for positive or negative indicators in the customer's manner and behavior. However, remember your first impression may not always be right. Don't become discouraged. The customer's negative attitude may be changeable if you respond in the right way. Stimulate the customer's desire to buy by offering different choices. However, don't do a hard sell and try to sell the customer things they don't want or need. They will resent that. Help the customer sift through many choices by listening to how they plan to use the product and advise what's best for the customer not for the store.

Brand names help make the sale for some products but not for others. Brand names are recognized for their consistent quality, unique design, durability and intangible values like appearance, reputation, satisfaction, comfort and fit. Brand names work for things like furniture, clothes, sunglasses and smart phones but not for plumbing supplies or lumber. If the brand is sufficiently well known, it will sell itself.

You haven't made a sale until you close and receive payment. Many salespeople have trouble closing. When the customer has considered all the choices and obviously prefers one, close by asking for the order and talking about delivery. If the customer wants to think about it, give them brochures and samples. Ask the customer if you may call the next day for their decision.

2-2 Q. My business's products are sold by direct outside sales. How can I increase my sales?

A.   Direct outside sales involve sales of things like insurance, investment products, real estate, repair and construction projects and equipment and furnishings. There are similarities to retail sales but also important differences. Your marketing plan identifies the potential customers but your sales staff have to make face to face sales calls to close the sales and produce revenue. The sales person must know everything about the product or service that the customer is likely to ask. Learn all you can about the customer's business and needs. Try to find a friend or acquaintance who knows the customer and can refer you to the customer. Even a referral by a casual acquaintance of you and the customer can make the difference in getting an appointment compared to a cold call. Having inventory on hand for immediate delivery may or may not be important depending on the product and situation.

A good initial contact is an introductory letter or brochure by mail describing your product or service and how it can help the customer. Say you will call for an appointment. Follow up with a phone call at a convenient time for the customer. Ask questions and listen to determine the customer's needs. Try to determine what they value most: low price-good quality-durability-service after the sale-reliability-choices-prompt delivery. Based on your previous experience with similar customers you may already know what to expect from the customer. Try to learn enough about the customer's needs to prepare a proposal for your first face to face sales call.

Go to your first sales call with a written proposal and prepared to close the sale. If possible, include in your proposal: prices-quality-delivery and models, drawings and layouts if appropriate. Remember customers are very busy people. They usually are looking for quality, reliability and completion on time with as little of their time and attention as possible. Meet their expectations and you are likely to get repeat orders.

When the customer has asked all their questions and appears satisfied with the proposal ask for a written order. The written order should clearly describe the project in terms of quality, quantities, price and delivery. That will avoid disputes later. The customer may want to think about it for a few days and shop around. If so, follow up with a phone call and ask for the order.

Often you will not have a referral and your first contact will by necessity be a cold call. It takes a lot of courage and self discipline to make cold calls. You may get rejected and rejection is painful. However, more likely you will be received with courtesy and maybe make a sale or start a relationship that leads to later sales.

2-3. Q. How important is it to sell online to supplement my storefront sales?

A. For many businesses selling online is very important and being found online is even more important. Nationally, online sales are only 6 percent of retail sales. However, online sales are growing 17 percent each year compared to about 3.5 percent for storefront sales.

Before online selling, a retailer wanting to sell products or services to a large local market of consumers had an impossible obstacle. The only way you can reach that many people with your message is with mass media like TV, radio and daily newspapers. Mass media costs way too much for small businesses.

Online marketing with websites, social media and smart phones is leveling the competition for small businesses. A professionally designed website or social media page has a onetime cost of about $500 to $1,000. The professional will make your website and social media page easily found on a customer search. Already 38 percent of customers find merchants with smart phone searches and that's growing rapidly. The professional will also teach you how to maintain and use the website and social media page.

Your website can be interactive and complete the sale with a service like PayPal. That enables you to sell online within, say, a radius of 200 miles. That's a large potential market.

You can use your local inventory to fill online orders to be delivered overnight by lower cost truck services. By comparison your large national online marketing competitors have to ship to that market area by overnight air freight through Louisville or Memphis which costs a lot more.

I know a florist who accepted orders by e-mail from out of town customers. He took a digital picture of the flower arrangement and after delivery e-mailed the picture to the customer saying this is the arrangement I delivered. That ability to visually share the experience got him repeat customers. You can do that now by smart phone.

You can probably handle more than 10 percent increase in sales from online customers without increasing inventory, labor, rent or utility costs. That means most of that online new sales revenue will go straight to your bottom-line profit.

2-4 Q. How can I get more customers for my freelance services?

A. Be cautious about searching for freelance work online. That tends to produce lowball bids and some opportunities may be unethical or frauds. Ask your existing clients for repeat business. Repeat customers are the core of most successful businesses. Successful businesses typically have two thirds or more repeat customers. Repeat customers know your work and have confidence in you. Stay in contact with your repeat customers and ask about upcoming projects and needs.

Ask repeat customers for referrals. A good goal is to have two thirds of your new customers be referrals by existing customers. Repeat customers are likely to know about the needs of other similar businesses. Network with prospective clients. That can be done by attending business events or participating in discussions in online networks. That provides an opportunity to interact with others on common interests and make an impression.

Potential networking opportunities are professional organizations in your area, Chambers of Commerce, Industry trade shows and conferences and websites that attract potential customers.

Network with fellow freelancers. Join trade associations and informal groups. Other freelancers may have overflow work and need help to meet schedule deadlines. Pitch agencies in your area. Many businesses outsource to agencies who in turn subcontract work to freelancers. Deliver speeches at trade shows and conferences in your area. That gets you before potential customers and establishes you as an expert.

Create partnerships. There's a demand for freelancers because large businesses are outsourcing more work. However, large businesses don't want the burden of managing large numbers of freelancers. Freelancers band together with others with complementary skills in what is referred to as "hives" to offer a comprehensive service. The hive provides the project management that the customer otherwise would have to handle. Hives should include related services that customers typically group together.

Hives need ground rules on who will be the project manager, joint billing, and division of the revenue.

Search reputable niche boards. Tell people how to do your work. That may sound counterproductive, why tell people how to do your job? They may elect to do it themselves. But many won't want to do that and will hire you if they think you're good. Turn down low paying work. Time spent in low paying work consumes time you could spend looking for or doing high paying work. However, if you're new in the market, some discounting may be necessary to establish your reputation. Freelancing is similar to job searches. You never know in advance what will pay off. Try everything to improve your odds.

2-5 Q. How can my business defend itself from online competition?

A. The best defense from online business is to be in the right kind of business. The right kinds of businesses are those that have inherent barriers to online competition. Examples of these are do-it-yourself (DIY) stores, dollar stores, restaurants, and pharmacies. DIY stores sell large, bulky items that are costly to ship and typically require technical help from the store staff to explain how to use the item to the customer.

Dollar stores sell low-cost items whose price is less than the online shipping costs. Online competitors can't compete because of shipping costs. Restaurants have competitive advantage because it's not possible to deliver quality hot food online. Pharmacies provide medicines that are needed immediately and can't wait for online delivery. Customers also often have questions for the pharmacist that can't be answered online.

Businesses that sell items the customer wants to see and touch before buying have a competitive advantage. That would include items like furniture, carpeting and window dressings. Clothing and shoes need to be tried on for correct fit and appearance. You never know how clothing will look on you until you try it on. You also never know how it will fit because standard sizes are not consistent enough, especially now with most clothing made overseas.

Local hardware stores have competitive advantage over online sales. Often the customer needs the item immediately and can't wait for online delivery. Also, the customer often needs advice from the salesclerk on how to use the item that can't be delivered online. Successful hardware stores have skilled, knowledgeable salesclerks who can answer customer questions. The same is true for plant nurseries. They have competitive advantage similar to hardware stores.

Businesses that sell items that require installation and follow on services have competitive advantages over online sales. Examples would be household appliances like refrigerators, dish washers, washing machines and dryers.

The return rate for many items sold online is very high, up to 70 percent of sales. That creates return shipping costs and re-stocking costs that local box stores don't have. Any items subject to the customer changing their mind after receiving it is better sold in local box stores.

Shopping for items like clothing, electronic devices and crafts is major entertainment for US shoppers. They don't get that pleasure form online shopping. Entertainment shopping often leads to impulse buying which online merchants can't compete with.

2-6 Q. How important is customer satisfaction in getting good customers to refer new customers?

A. Good customer referrals and endorsements is more effective in getting new customers than any form of advertising. However, the effectiveness of customer referrals depends on your industry and your business situation. Effectiveness of customer referrals depends on the following 3 questions:

*Does the purchase involve a significant investment? If it does the customer faces significant risk if they make the wrong choice of a supplier. As a result, the customer is likely to consult with friends to find a recommended supplier and is likely to follow the recommendation. If it doesn't, the customer has little risk if they choose the wrong supplier and may not seek out a referral.

*Is there sufficient published information available to the customer to help them make a good choice? There are product rating systems available for some products and customer ratings on websites. The Better Business Bureau provides ratings for businesses. Generally, the less reliable information available means that customer referrals are more important and effective. Examples are consumer services like auto mechanics and home repair services.

*How frequently are consumers in the market for that product or service? Customers are more likely to remember good customer referrals if they buy the product or service often. If they buy the product infrequently, the customer has to ask friends for referrals which is less likely. Generally, referrals are more effective if the product or service is bought often.

It's generally thought that dissatisfied customers are more likely to make bad recommendations and satisfied customers are less likely to make good recommendations. That's true to some degree. Customers rated 1 for satisfaction are twice as likely to make a bad recommendation as a customer rated 10 is likely to make a good recommendation. Customers rated 5-7 are basically satisfied and are not likely to make either bad or good recommendations.

However, with that said, you really can't afford dissatisfied 1-4 customers. They can be very emotional and vocal about their perceived poor treatment and can cause great damage to the business's reputation. That's true especially with social media where their bad mouthing can be sent to hundreds or thousands quickly. It's worth the time, effort and expense to try to resolve their complaint quickly.

2-7 Q. Is discounting a good marketing strategy?

A. Yes, if done right. No, if done wrong. Never discount just to make a sale. Discount to make a profitable sale or at least a future profitable sale to that customer. Discounting is only profitable if the business already has enough sales revenue to pay all maintenance and operating costs and be profitable or at least break even. Then if the business discounts to make an additional incremental sale, 100 percent of that sale revenue goes directly to profit because previous sales dollars have already paid the maintenance and operating costs.

The most profitable discount sale is for a distinct product that is also time sensitive. A good example is a hotel's sale of its last room for a specific date or a cruise ship's sale of its last cabin for a specific date. The product is distinct because it's for a specific date and it's time sensitive because if not sold the room or cabin becomes of zero value to the business. All sales revenue goes straight to profit but if not sold the profit is zero. That's why customers can get great discount deals at the last minute. Similar sales are entertainment event tickets, air travel tickets and perishable produce at grocery stores.

The second most profitable discount sale is for larger orders. A good example is a widget maker who had capacity to make 1,000 widgets per day. Most businesses can increase sales by 10 percent without any increase in maintenance and operating costs. If the widget maker has orders for only 1,000 widgets per day and gets an offer for an extra 100 widgets per day at a 10 percent discount, he takes it, because his extra maintenance and operating costs for the extra 100 widgets is zero. All sales revenue for the extra 100 goes straight profit, Except for cost of goods sold. The same would be true if the widget maker offered the existing customers 10 percent more widgets at a 10 percent discount.

The third most profitable discount sales are for standing orders or for repeat sales. If the widget maker can sell 700 widgets per day on standing orders and to reliable repeat customers with a small discount, its worthwhile to run at full capacity, make the 700 widgets and store them until the customer takes delivery. Otherwise, the widget maker would have to reduce production to 300 widgets per day which would be inefficient and costly and the opportunity to produce and sell the 700 widgets would be lost forever.

The fourth most profitable discount for a retail business is to sell off slow moving merchandise and replace it with fast selling merchandise. Sales display space is a retailer's most valuable asset. The retailer needs to maximize sales revenue from each square foot of display space.

2-8 Q. What is a good marketing plan for starting a new business selling low-cost items to retail customers?

A. It's tough to market low-cost items or services to retail customers. Your marketing message must reach a very large number of consumers in a geographical market area to sell enough products at competitive prices to cover overhead expenses and profit. That's difficult and expensive to do. First, you usually have competitors who share the market. Each competitor can only expect to get a portion of the market. Second, your competitors are already known by the customers. You're not. The existing competitors typically get more than two thirds of their sales from repeat customers and two thirds of their new customers through referrals by their existing customers. It will likely take you 6 to 12 months to reach that level of repeat customers and new referral customers.

The following are relatively low cost and effective marketing strategies. Advertise in local bi-weekly, weekly and twice a week newspaper. Their rates are much lower than daily newspapers and their readers are more focused on the contents. Run repeat ads often. Potential customers usually have to see the ad at least 6 times before it penetrates their consciousness. Use the ads to offer introductory discounts. Join the chamber of commerce or local business association and request a grand opening ribbon cutting. Offer the attendees introductory discounts.

Offer regular discounts to repeat customers and to large volume customers like buy ten and get one free. Ask related businesses and service organizations to refer customers by distributing your sales promotion materials. Potential referral sources depending on your type product might be apartment buildings, property management offices, realtors, RV parks, motels and other businesses. Offer discounts or prizes to existing customers who refer new customers. Remember your goal is to reach two thirds repeat customers and two thirds new customer referrals as quick as possible.

Have a well-designed website with your location, contact information, product description and product pictures, prices and useful information about your products. Update the website regularly with new content. Make sure your website design and key words bring up your website as high as possible on the first page of online searches. Make sure smart phone and GPS searches will find your website. Distribute marketing brochures door to door. Have good signage. Select a location that will generate walk in customers. Locate near a business that attracts customers who will also need your products. For example, if your business is a pet grooming service locate near a veterinary office and ask the veterinarian to refer customers. Get the best possible prices from your suppliers. Don't overlook or neglect any part of your market. Try to make your products better than competitor's and equal in price. During startup expect to spend a lot on marketing to get repeat customers.

2-9 Handling Customer complaints

Q. My retail store customer complaints have increased, what can I do to reduce them?

A. How the complaint is handled is the key to customer satisfaction. Typically, only 37 percent are satisfied with a monetary solution to the complaint. However, 74 percent are satisfied after receiving both a monetary solution and an explanation or apology. Because of today's fast pace of life customers want a resolution and they want it fast.

Typically, it cost 5 times as much to get a new customer as it does to retain an existing customer. There is a high risk of losing an existing customer if their complaint is not resolved to their satisfaction. With today's internet and social media, it is more urgent than ever to resolve complaints quickly. About 35 percent of customers post their complaint on social media and the internet thus multiplying the potential damage many times. Social media and internet empower customers to fight back when they feel wronged.

There are best practices for handling complaints. First, make it easy for customers to register their complaints promptly and easily. Some store managers and owners put their business phone number on each sales receipt. Second, train sales staff to properly handle complaints. For staff that regularly handle complaints that could require 2 weeks training including training on how to diffuse anger and express empathy. Third, have clear policies for employees handling complaints stating their authority and options to resolve complaints. If necessary, the manager or owner should handle the complaint. Fourth, recognize the customer is always right even if it turns out they were wrong and caused the complaint. Humans make mistakes but will not be happy if they are told so.

Fifth, keep a log of each customer's complaint by name, type complaint and resolution. That will indicate repeat customer complaints and trends in the type of complaint which should trigger corrective action. Sixth, if the complaint is online or on social media, take it offline immediately and resolve it by telephone or if necessary, face to face. When resolved, post the resolution online so that customers know it was resolved satisfactorily. Seventh, recognize that saying we are human and made a mistake is not enough. The customer wants it fixed. Eighth, if the customer makes an unreasonable demand in excess of the store's policy, do not say no outright. Offer an alternative. However, do not get into an argument with the customer. Simply say this is our store's policy in this situation and this is all we can offer.

2-10 Competing with Online Marketing

Q. It seems my retail store can't compete with the online marketers. Are retain stores doomed to become extinct?

A. Retail stores are here to stay. Total retail sales in 2016 (excluding restaurants, gasoline, and automobiles) was $3.4 trillion nationwide. Of that, online sales were only 11 percent or about $400 billion. Online sales are growing faster than instore sales. Shopping center space is overbuilt in the US and will decline.

To survive and even flourish, retail stores must provide "emotional fulfillment" to the customer. By that I mean the joy customers take in seeing, touching, sniffing, and testing the product before they buy. Online retailers can't provide that experience.

Even the successful online marketers are building retail stores. They need to connect and fuse with customers face to face to understand what customers want.

A good strategy for successful retail in store sales is make the retail store an appealing place to visit with free parking and well qualified sales staff who know their products and know how to please the customer. Spend time every day on the retail floor watching and chatting with customers and you will be amazed by the intelligence you pick up from them.

Provide a variety of experiences for the customer. During the Christmas shopping season, have special holiday events. Provide a variety of retail stores to satisfy the needs of all customers.

Obviously, single retail stores can't match a shopping mall with large scale entertainment; however, there are smaller things that would create a pleasant shopping experience such as free coffee, music or a small art gallery.

2-11 Keeping Customers Loyal

Q. How important is customer satisfaction in keeping customers loyal?

A. Customer satisfaction is one critical factor in customer loyalty but not the only one. The impact of customer satisfaction on loyalty is different for each business depending on its situation. One system rates customer satisfaction on a scale from 1 to 10 with 1 being poorest and 10 being best.

First there is a huge difference between what customers say (intended loyalty) and what they do (actual loyalty). For low satisfaction customers (1-4) there is a big difference of 25 percent between intended loyalty and actual loyalty. For high satisfaction customers (10), there are no differences between intended loyalty and actual loyalty. Both are about 50 percent. That means that the other loyalty factors are critical to retaining the low satisfaction customers and not critical to the high satisfaction customers.

The first other factor is the number of competitors you have. The more competitors you have the easier and more likely your customers will switch. If there are no competitors, you have a monopoly, and the threat is zero. The other factors relate to the cost of switching in dollars, effort, and risk. The second factor is frequency of purchase. If the customer buys the product weekly, there's little risk of making a bad choice. If the purchase is a household appliance with a 10-year life, there's a lot of risk if the choice is bad.

The third factor is availability of information about the alternative product. Nowadays there's a lot of third-party product ratings, like for cars and consumer guides for numerous products. There's also the internet with a world of information about products.

The fourth factor is product cost. Customers can afford to take risks of a bad choice on a low-cost product of $100 or less. There is a lot of risk in buying a car or major household appliance if the choice is bad.

Customer loyalty is critical for any business because it typically costs 5 times as much to recruit a new customer as it does to retain a repeat customer. Although there are other factors contributing to customer loyalty, customer satisfaction is the single most critical factor. Loyal, repeat customers not only reduce your marketing costs, but also provide a dependable revenue to pay your business expenses and refer new customers to you.

2-12 Repeat Customer Marketing

Q. How important are repeat customers to my business?

A. When I help clients with their marketing plan, I use the two thirds rule. For an existing successful business, they should strive for at least two thirds repeat customers who typically will spend two thirds more than a onetime customer and two thirds of their new customers should be referred by satisfied repeat customers.

That means that repeat customers produce most of the business's sales revenue. That's the competitive advantage an existing business has over a startup. The startup has no repeat customers, and it takes time to build that customer base.

To use repeat customer marketing most effectively you need to be selling a product or service customers need often like weekly or bi-weekly. Once you get them in your door and make a sale you have a good chance to repeat that sale often.

By comparison a real estate agent or new car dealership makes a sale maybe every 5 to 10 years. That takes forever to establish a reliable repeat customer base. Location is important in getting repeat customers. For example, if you sell household items that a grocery store doesn't sell that are needed often, locating near the grocery store would be very advantageous.

You create repeat customers by focusing on your competitive advantages. All businesses compete based on price, quality and service. It's difficult to excel in all three. Find out which one or two your customers care most about and focus on that. In some cases convenience is a customer priority.

For example, I live on North Padre Island. In recent years we got our first pharmacy and hardware store. The closest competition is 10 or more miles away. Those stores are doing great. Sometimes choices are important as with new car dealerships and restaurant menus.

Special discounts for repeat customers is a powerful tool to build your repeat customer base. Special discounts to repeat customers for each new customer they refer is also effective. 89 percent of shoppers for necessities like food look for discounts. About a third of consumer-packaged goods sell on discounts and those discounts can be 30 to 50 percent.

Get to know your repeat customers by name and their interests. Provide useful information about how to use your product. For example, if I owned a plant nursery, I'd collect my customers e-mail addresses and send a monthly e-mail newsletter with current seasonal information and tips about planting, insect control, fertilizing, watering and pruning.

I'd do likewise on my business website and social media page. That establishes you as a creditable, trustworthy source of information and causes your repeat customers to rely on you and return when they need your kind of products or services.

2-13 Data Driven Marketing

Q. What is data driven marketing and how do I use it in my business?

A. Once upon a time, small businesses could know their customers personally and recognize their likes and dislikes. First, malls drew customers from a wide area, then online marketing made customers global. It's very difficult now to know your customers.

Collecting and utilizing data about customers tells you who they are, where they live, and their purchasing behavior. Data driven marketing is the process to obtain insights and trends by analyzing company generated or market data and use the data to design your marketing plan. To use data driven marketing collect information on all aspects of your customers engagement with you.

Then use the data to design your marketing plan with the objective to get the best return on investment (ROI) from your marketing investment. Your objective is to learn who your customers are, what they buy and don't buy and why they buy form you. That tells you what products to stock or not stock and who to direct your marketing to. However, don't let the numbers interfere with your creativity and inventiveness in marketing. The process requires, planning (set your marketing goals), test strategies (on a small scale), analyze results (measure results), iterate (try another strategy), deploy (do it), scale up (if it works).

There are a lot of tools available to gather data, one source lists 37 must have tools, you probably will need professional help to choose the best tools for your business.

When you set marketing goals and implement action plans and strategies its critical to design a way to measure results. Otherwise you don't know what works and what doesn't work. You can't improve what you don't measure. Try to find tools that measure results of your different marketing strategies. That's the only way to know your (ROI) on the money you spend on a marketing strategy.

2-14 Determining if a Customer Will Buy

Q. I have a great idea for a new product. How can I determine whether customers will buy it?

A. As the old saying goes "You have the cart before the horse." When you set out to invent a new, successful product or service, first ask "What is the unfilled customer need? How many customers have that need?" Is it thousands, tens of thousands or millions and tens of millions? More is better because that determines the potential size of the market and potential profit. Second, think of as many ideas as possible to fill that need. Third, screen and evaluate each idea for a product or service. There's a long list of questions to ask about each idea: *Why would customers choose it? *Is it sustainable? *What benefits does it deliver to the customer? *Are the benefits unique and different from others? *What value does it bring to the customer? *Will the customer be willing to pay enough to cover the cost-plus profit? When evaluating ideas for products or services, remember that customers don't buy a product or service. Instead, they buy a solution to a problem.

There's also a list of questions about your potential customer: *Who are your customers? *Are they all ages, genders and income levels or subsectors of the general population? *Is your customer a consumer, business or nonprofit? If it is a business, then ask who does the buying and what, why, when, and how do they buy? Often the person who writes the purchase order for a business or nonprofit is not the person who decides what to buy and from which supplier. Those decisions are usually made by the end user of the product or service. *If the customer is a consumer, then ask who actually makes the buying decision, the father, mother or child.

The result of the above screening and evaluation process is to determine whether there is a market opportunity for your best idea for a new product or service. Ideas are plentiful, but market opportunities are rare. To be a market opportunity the idea must *solve a customer's urgent problem for millions or tens of millions of customers. * have customer growth potential *create large profit potential for you the inventor. That means you must be able to produce the product or service at a cost the customer is willing to pay for a solution to that problem and leave a good profit margin for you. There are numerous examples of new products and services that failed because they were not cost effective. Supersonic jet passenger service between the US and Europe failed because it was not cost effective. It met customers need for shorter travel time, but cost was prohibitive.

Most inventors of new products and services don't have the skills set to do the required R&D, produce it, distribute, and market it. Those functions require the skills of a CEO, CFO, and COO.

2-15 Getting and retaining customer for Service Business

Q. How can my service business get repeat customers and new customer referrals?

A. Service businesses should use the two thirds strategy. Meaning two thirds of its customers should be repeat customers and two thirds of new customers should be referred by existing customers. It's even better if it's eighty percent rather than two thirds. That's the reason new businesses are at a competitive disadvantage. They don't have the repeat customer base and it takes time to build that base.

First you must produce good quality, timely, and convenient services at competitive prices. If the customer comes to your business site and waits for the service, have a comfortable waiting area that is clean, well painted, and well lighted with TV, reading material, coffee/soft drink machine and now days, consider WiFi. The counter persons should be knowledgeable with good people skills and sales skills.

After the service is complete, the service technician should tell the customer what was done and why and answer any questions. That makes the customer feel that they have received good value for their money. Call the customer 3 days after the service during the evening and ask for their performance feedback by rating the service as satisfactory, good, excellent. Send an email to the customer 90 days after the service thanking them and ask if they need additional service. Consider sending the customer email newsletters quarterly with useful information and tips about your services. That serves as a reminder and the customer will remember your business when they need additional service.

Most service businesses offer some kind of free service to repeat customers as a reward for their business. It doesn't need to be a high-cost service, just something they will value and appreciate. For example, a tire business could offer free rotation. An auto mechanic service could offer a free safety inspection or free installation of car tag stickers or free fluid level checks. Give the repeat customer a discount voucher of, say, $5, $10 or $15 on the next service. Some new car agencies offer free oil change service for the first 2 years. After 2 years they expect the customer will be likely to continue getting their services there.

New customers often find their service provider by asking for referrals from friends and relatives. Offer repeat customers a discount voucher of, say, $25 on their next service for referring a friend to your business. Offer new first-time customers a discount on their first service.

2-16 Good Networking Practices

Q. What are good networking practices?

A. Networking is not about passing out as many business cards as possible in the shortest time possible. It's about forming long term relationships with others who you can help and in return they will help you. You are looking for mutual support and benefit.

Don't network aimlessly. Before going to a networking session decide what type of relationship you are seeking. It could be new customers, suppliers, sources of information, advisors, sources of capital, potential business partners or customer referrals.

Expect to help the other person first. That creates leverage. The other person will appreciate your help and will reciprocate later when you need help. Don't expect to benefit immediately. Be patient. Your goal is to establish a long-term relationship and that takes time.

Be the first to arrive. A few early arrivals standing around a large room feel awkward and a little apprehensive. That creates a good situation to break the ice and start a conversation. Stay late. It's easier to start a conversation when there are fewer people present.

If your industry sponsors a charity event, volunteer to help. The time you spend planning and staging events and raising contributions will be appreciated by those you work with who may be useful relationships later. You establish a common experience in working for a good cause that you and others feel good about.

Volunteer to speak on panels at conferences. That establishes you as a creditable source of information. Others will want to meet you. After meeting a new person follow up with useful information that may interest them. Don't try too hard to impress initially. Let the relationship develop at a natural pace.

Successful networkers use a stepwise process when meeting new people. First, start with an opening comment about the shared environment. It could be about a speaker, program or even about the weather. Second, introduce yourself and give hints about the topics you'd like to talk about or topics the other person might want to talk about. Third, ask questions to find a topic both want to discuss. Avoid your favorite topics. You would tend to dominate the conversation.

Look for common interests and experiences. Those will form an instant bond between you. Fourth, proceed with caution. The trick is for both to avoid talking too much or too much about a single topic. If the other person is talking too much, change the topic.

Fifth, make a graceful exit. Exchange business cards and say you will keep in touch.

2-17 Marketing New Products

Q. I have developed a great quality new product customers will love. How do I market it?

A. In one case an entrepreneur produced great quality meats with his special seasoning that tasted better. He had been successful in the local market but wanted to grow by marketing online. However, he didn't have a marketing plan. Investors know that having a great quality produce by itself is not enough. You must have a way to tell your story to customers and have them recognize and want to buy the quality product.

Ask yourself how will potential customers recognize the quality of my product? For meats, the customer will judge it on taste. That means you must get the meat in the customers hands to taste. The best way to do that is with free samples. The entrepreneur had done that successfully locally.

His pitch to the investors should have been I want to sell X percent of my company for Y dollars. I will use the investment to finance shipping free samples to online potential customers. My local marketing indicates that 10 percent of potential customers who try my meats will become regular, repeat customers, and will spend an average of Z dollars each year. I will use the net profit of 20 percent on those sales to send more free samples and repeat the process until my sales plateau, indicating I've reached the maximum share of market for my business. Then I will start returning profits to my investors and consider an Initial Public Offering (IPO) to allow investors to cash out if they wish. I estimate the IPO will occur in 5 years.

Customers recognize the quality of products in different ways depending on the nature of the product. In some cases, a picture of the product may be sufficient. Personal appearance products use before and after pictures to show the benefits of use. A video showing how the product works and is used may work for some products. Use the physical senses of sight, smell, taste and feel if you can.

Customers love to experience the products quality advantages. Written testimonials by satisfied customers are good. Testimonials are especially good make by a recognized expert in that field, such as a professional golfer endorsing a new golf club.

The key to success of a new, better-quality product is the marketing, not the product itself. You must tell customers why the product is better and convince them.

2-18 Establishing Brand Name

Q. How can I establish my business as a brand?

A. If 2 percent of your customers are loyal repeat customers, they can contribute 20 percent of sales and drive 80 percent of sales with their recommendations and endorsements. Rule #1: Don't ask your customers what they want because they don't know. Instead show them.

Rule #2: Woo your biggest fans because they are worth it. Your 2 percent loyal customers can produce 20 percent of sales but be responsible for 80 percent of sales through their advocating to friends and acquaintances. One loyal customer can create many other loyal customers who in turn can create still more.

Rule #3: Welcome your customer's complaints. A complainer is emotionally involved. If you can satisfy them, they are likely to become loyal customers. Listen, find out what the real complaint is. Be polite and thankful. Fix it to the customer's satisfaction and don't let it happen again.

Rule#4: Looks and appearance do count.

Rule #5: Transform your employees into passionate disciples who love their jobs. The key words are listening, helping, engaging, suggesting. Passion is infectious and stimulates a similar response from customers.

Rule #6: Ramp up your virtual relationships with customers online. That means frequent good communication with customers online with helpful information they need and appreciate. Customers with the most disposable income have the least amount of time and use the internet to efficiently use that time.

Rule #7: Take giant leaps because you're not going to win with timid steps. Most businesses strive for continuous improvement and incremental advances followed by consolidation. However, that strategy won't produce rapid growth. I once had a retail client who expanded their sales space by 3 times in one step. I cautioned a more deliberate pace, but it worked.

Rule #8: Find out what schizogenesis means to save your customer relationships. It's an anthropology term meaning relationships are not stable. Brands are always moving up or down not stable. Once they start down, it's hard to turn them around. Loyal customers can help you a lot, but if you disappoint them, they can hurt you a lot, especially with social media.

2-19 Marketing to Millennials

Q. Is marketing to Millennials different than other generations?

A. Yes, according to one study, it is. The Millennial generation is those presently between age 18 and 34. Millennials spend about $1.3 Trillion annually. Of that about $430 Billion is for discretionary, nonessential things. By 2030 Millennials are projected to outnumber baby boomers 78 million to 56 million. Millennial spending will increase rapidly because of their increasing numbers and increasing incomes as they age.

Millennials' shopping preferences and buying habits are developing now and they are different from other generations. They have different product and service preferences, values, personalities and outlook on life. They engage with the companies they buy from more extensively, personally and emotionally. They expect a two-way mutual relationship with the companies they buy from.

They communicate with electronic devices online, smart phones, tablets and social media. Through electronic communications they influence the purchases of other generations. If they like your product or service, they will promote your business to large numbers of friends on social media. However, if they don't like your products or services, they will quickly bad mouth you to those same large numbers of friends. That kind of criticism can quickly go viral and is very difficult to combat or re-butt.

Millennials have high expectations of businesses they buy from. They expect the business to help those in need, be socially responsible, be good environmental stewards, protect their customer's data and be transparent and sincere. They like to feel they are doing good by buying your product or service.

Millennials are not receptive to advertising by mass media like radio, TV, and newspapers. Instead, they like to hear from you by online, smart phone, tablets, and social media. Those enable them to communicate with your business and their friends interactively. They expect that 50 percent of your communication with them will be a conversation about their likes and shared comments.

They expect another 30 percent to be useful information and tips about what you know that they don't know but will find useful or interesting. Only 20 percent of your communication should be about your business where you offer new products or services and make calls to action to take advantage of discounts and sales. They want short communications on a single topic. They like topics that prompt them to comment on the topic with their friends.

Millennial's preference for online, smart phones, tablets and social media communications is an advantage for small businesses. Those media are relatively inexpensive compared to mass media. Most small businesses can't afford mass media while large businesses can. Learn to communicate with them electronically with conversation, information and tips that attract their interest and devote the necessary time to do so regularly.

2-20 New Consumer Product

Q. I have invented a new consumer product that customers will love and buy. What problems can I expect?

A. You have an almost insurmountable obstacle. First, selling consumer products is one of the most difficult things in business. For example, if you want to sell consumer products to all 300,000 residents in your market, the only way to reach that many people with your message is by mass media like TV, radio and newspapers. That's the reason candidates for elective office use mass media blitzes to appeal to voters.

However, mass media costs way too much for a startup business or to introduce a new product or service. In recent years, website online marketing and social media marketing offer an affordable alternative. But you must be expert in how to use those media successfully. Also, only certain kinds of products or services sell well online and on social media. It's not likely you could sell any generic product or service, like plumbing supplies, online or on social media. It needs to be a product or service that appeals to customers interest or curiosity.

Second, it's impossible to tell whether customers will like and buy your product until you produce it and sell it in a test market. It's irrelevant that you are convinced customers will love and buy it. You never, ever know that for sure until you test market it.

One of the first questions investors ask is "how many have you sold in what kinds of markets and what was your revenues"? That is also what an "angel" investor will ask. They know from personal experience you can't know whether customers will buy it until you try it. It helps if you have successfully sold similar products to consumers. If you haven't sold similar products to consumers,
you have no basis to say customers will buy it. It may seem logical that customers should need it, want it and buy it. However, what you think they need, want and should buy may make no sense to the customer.

I had a client one time who had picked a location for a full-service car wash that he was convinced would be a slam dunk, guaranteed success. All he needed was about $1 million to build it. He had no experience in the car wash business and therefore, had no basis for thinking customers would use it. There is never a slam dunk, guaranteed success in business. Sometimes location can be a key to success. A pharmacy or Hardware store in a remote area with 10,000 residents are an example of that.

2-21 Customer Self Service

Q. How far should my business go to "customer self-serve" to reduce costs?

A. Customer self-serve is a two-edged sword. Many retailers have gone to self-check-out. Banks encourage online banking and reduce branches. You can shop online for travel arrangements and book your own tickets and hotel rooms. You buy your plane ticket online, print your boarding pass, weigh, and tag your luggage and put it on the conveyor. Call centers direct you through a long process to get your information or do a transaction. One reason so many people feel over worked is because of the time and attention they spend on self-service.

For some things self-service is more convenient and better for the customer. Printing boarding passes is one example. It is better than the alternative of waiting to be served. Filing your IRS tax return electronically is probably better than dealing with IRS on a paper return. For those who can afford to pay more, there are special pampered services that eliminate self-service. Many hospitals now offer valet parking. You can download movies at home rather than rent one at a storefront. One download service uses a TV ad showing a frustrated customer repeatedly trying to self-check-out a movie.

There is a downside for businesses. If they take self-service too far, customers learn to comparative price shop and buy based on lowest price. That drives the profit margin to a minimum for the business. Customers who buy on lowest price will not be loyal repeat customers. If the business's staff never meet the customer, the business loses touch with what the customer wants and values. The business cannot differentiate itself based on good service or quality. The business cannot build a continuing relationship with the customer.

The business loses the opportunity to sell the customer something else. Businesses go to great effort and expense to get the customer to physically visit their store. They know that once there, the customer is likely to buy other items. It creates the opportunity for impulse purchases.

Self-service cannot handle problems and special situations. We have all had frustration with call centers when the staff person did not have the know-how or experience to handle our problem or options offered did not solve our problem.

With all the negatives, self-service is a great cost cutter. For many transactions it cuts the cost by many times. Use it where it works well, but not for everything.

2-22 Limiting Returns

Q. My retail business has a high return rate by customers. Should I limit returns by customers?

A. Not accepting returns by retail customers is a tricky issue that you probably need expert outside help with. Unhappy customers could create a viral volume of critical reports about the business on social media. There are services that will monitor your customers return behavior and create a "risk score" for each customer. You could set criteria from the risk score at which the service would warn customers that continued returns could result in rejection or the criteria for rejecting returns. A recent survey estimated retailers lost $351 billion in sales returns last year and $22.8 billion of that came from fraudulent and abusive returns. That would indicate about 6.5 percent of returns are suspect. Total annual retail sales are about $3.4 trillion, so the total return rate is about 10.3 percent. You would need to compile your own business records to determine how serious the problem is and whether it's serious enough to risk losing customers.

One service bases its customer "risk score" on the following types of customer return behavior?
- Returning a large percentage of total purchases
- Returning a high dollar amount
- Returning items without a receipt
- Returning items that tend to get stolen at the retailer
- Returning an item after a certain period
- Returning too many items in a short period
- Returning an item just before store closing time

In addition, there are common sense criteria such as returning items after obvious considerable use.

Rather than dealing with returns, consider ways to prevent customers from buying items that are likely to be returned. For example, when customers buy items such as clothing for others, try to ensure that the customer knows the person's correct size or preference in colors and styles. Try to guide the customer to make the correct choice. Other examples would be to try to ensure the customer knows how to use the item or to install the item which is often the case with hardware store merchandise. If the sales staff takes time to explain how the item is used or installed, that could prevent unnecessary returns.

It would be worthwhile to list the items that are frequently returned and analyze how the sales staff could have avoided the customer's wrong choice. Effort spent avoiding returns is a good business investment because it avoids the customer's frustration, disappointment and time spent making the return which should result in better customer satisfaction, which is very valuable for your business. It also avoids your restocking and resale costs.

2-23 Hiring A Sales-Person

Q. What are good qualifications to look for in hiring a salesperson?

A. There are 6 qualifications to look for. First, a good listener. They sell more by talking less. You detect that in the interview by how much the candidate talks and how they encourage you to talk by asking good questions. Second, authenticity and honesty. It's good for a salesperson to be able to think on their feet, but it's not good to fake it when they don't know the answer. For better to admit they don't have the answer and promise to get it. Third, research skills. That means knowing how to research the customers business before making a sales call. Give the candidate basic information about a customer and ask them to research the business and give you a report prior to the job offer.

Fourth, Does the candidate know the competition? Good candidates will have researched your business and your competitors before they interview. Good salespersons know the competition. Otherwise, they won't know how to compete with the competition to get sales. That includes knowing the competitor's products and services and how well the competitor competes in the market. All businesses compete based on price, quality, and service. In addition, in some cases, convenience and choices are competitive areas. The salesperson should know which among price, quality and service is most valued by the customers and focus on those.

Fifth, Does the candidate know the market? A good salesperson can talk on most any topic and is well informed on current events. It's especially important that they know your industry and your local market. Each market is different. It's important to know whether the market is thriving or slow and the trends of what's selling and what's not selling. It's a big asset if the salesperson knows the customers personally and has a good reputation and relationship with the customers. Customers buy from those they know and trust.

Sixth, Is the candidate trustworthy? That's hard to determine in an interview. However, after the interview make notes on your perception of the candidate trustworthiness. Your perception is probably the same as the customers. Check the candidate's references, especially if the reference is a customer.

Regardless how thorough you are in the hiring process, you can be wrong. Train the salesperson well in your business and monitor and coach them for several months. Introduce them to your customers and make a smooth transition from the previous salesperson to the new.

2-24 What do my Customers Want?

Q. What do my customers want most from my business?

A. The answer to that question depends on your industry, product or service and your customers. All customers value price, quality and service. Many customers will also value reliability, choices, convenience, and value for the money. It's critical for each business to determine which of those your customers value most and to focus your efforts on excelling in those. A business can't excel in all areas. For example, it's not likely a business can have the best quality and the lowest price. Quality, typically, cost more. However, it's wasteful to provide best quality if your customer is mostly concerned about price.

Determining what your customers value most is not easy. It helps if you have worked in that industry and market for a long time and know the customers well. To find out what the customer values most, you must ask in face to face conversations or in customer surveys. Customer complaints is a valuable source of information. What the customer complains about clearly indicates what they value most.

On typical surveys asking for the three things customers care about most, about 70 percent say quality of the product or service. About 67 percent say value of the product or service for the money. About 41 percent say customer service. When asked how they evaluate the business, 74 percent say personal experience with the business. About another 59 percent say referrals by family, friends, and colleagues that they trust. Only 23 percent rely on the business's advertising and 15 percent on the business's website information.

Your business's results could be very different depending on the market and type product or service. For a residential roofing or home repair contractor, quality, reliability, and price are probably key values. The customer will probably rely on referrals by other satisfied customers. For a critical service, like plumbing, reliability and prompt service would be valued most. Groceries are probably bought based on price and quality. Some products, like gasoline, are made to standard quality specifications and sell primarily based on price.

For products like clothing and new car dealerships, choice would be highly valued by customers. In remote locations convenience would be highly valued to avoid having to drive many miles to the closest competitor store.

Since customers evaluate businesses based on personal experience and referrals by others, it's critical that a business always satisfy the customer if possible. Now days, a bad customer report can circulate by social media to hundreds or thousands of other customers in a few hours.

CHAPTER THREE

FINANCIAL PLANNING AND MANAGEMENT

SUMMARY

- Cash is king. If you run out of cash or credit to pay bills when due, you fail.
-
- Despite late night TV and radio ads, there is no free money, only loans.
-
- If you sell on terms, there is no cash sale until you collect.
-
- Get a bank loan line of credit while the business is thriving. You cannot get it when the business is in trouble and needs it.

CHAPTER THREE
FINANCIAL PLANNING AND MANAGEMENT

3-1 Financial Statements   64
3-2 Small Business Bank Loans
3-3 Bank Loan Applications
3-4 Getting Start-up Financing
3-5 Sources for Working Capital
3-6 Protection against Disasters
3-7 Preparing 5-year Strategic Plan
3-8 Selling Shares by Crowd Funding
3-9 Alternative Financing
3-10 Good Use of Investment Capital
3-11 Using Business Credit Cards

3-1 Financial Statements

Q. How important are financial statements in managing my business?

A. Extremely. Financial statements measure the success of your business. Without them you don't know how well or bad the business is doing until the cash runs out and then it's too late. I have had clients call for help whose business is about to go bankrupt. Unfortunately, at that late point, it's usually too late to help. Good financial statements would have predicted bankruptcy in advance when corrective actions could have been taken to avoid it. Another valuable use of financial statements is that they help you improve the business's profitability. Without financial measurement, you never know what strategies work and what doesn't. You want to continue what works and drop what doesn't add to the bottom line.

Basic financial statements include an annual 12- month budget and a 3-5 year strategic plan. The annual budget projects the sales revenue, cost of goods sold, expenses and profit for each month of the year. Your bookkeeper should calculate the actual sales revenue, cost of goods sold, expenses and profit for each month and compare it to the budget to show whether the business is on track. Look for the causes and try to correct if it is not. Without a comparison between projected and actual, you could be months too late realizing you have a problem. For new startup businesses, it's especially difficult to project realistic monthly sales revenue. That's the reason many new businesses fail.

The 3–5 year strategic plan projects annual sales revenue, cost of goods sold, expenses and profits. Its major benefit is in trying to anticipate major changes in business conditions that will impact the business either positively or negatively, so that you can plan for those changes.

Another valuable financial statement is the monthly cash flow statement. Prepare a projected cash flow statement annually for each 12 months showing cash revenue and cash disbursements. Have your bookkeeper produce actual monthly cash revenue and disbursements and compare it to the projections. Having cash on hand or credit available to pay bills as they come due is critical. Businesses go bankrupt when there's no cash or credit to pay bills. If you think you might need credit at some point during the year, get it early while the business is still thriving. You can't get it when the business is out of cash and desperate.

Monitor your gross margin as compared to your industry. Gross margin is sales revenue less cost of goods sold. If your gross margin is 30 percent and the industry average is 40 percent, you have a serious problem. That means either your prices are too low or you are paying too much for your merchandise if you are a retailer, or your raw material if you are a manufacturer or processor.

3-2 Small Business Bank Loans

Q. Can small business owners get bank loans?

A. Recent studies indicate many small business owners don't apply for bank loans for fear of rejection. About one out of two small businesses need credit but about 18 to 37 percent don't apply for fear of rejection. About a third to two thirds of those who didn't apply would have been approved had they applied. About 3 out of 4 startups receive some kind of credit funding during their first year. Startups that get a loan in the business's name are about 25 percent more likely to survive 3 years than those that get loans in their owner's name. Those that do survive 3 years have revenue about 50 to 110 percent greater than those that don't. The better survival rate with loans in the business's name probably means the business was more credit worthy to qualify for loans in its own name and the banks are more proactive monitoring and mentoring the business because repayment depends on its success.

Businesses can improve their chance for bank credit by having a good business plan. The business plan is a blueprint of everything important about the business including sales revenue, expenses, profit, and a balance sheet showing its assets and liabilities. Many small business owners don't think a business plan is worth the effort to prepare. However, the chance of getting a bank loan without the business plan and good financial statements is low. They provide the bank the necessary information to judge the business' ability to repay the loan.

The loan application should also state clearly what the credit will be used for. It could be to buy new more productive labor-saving equipment which would make the business more profitable. It could be to finance business growth that requires more working capital for more employees, space, or inventory. For contracting businesses, it could be for working capital to enable the business to take on more or larger projects.

Banks normally expect to lend 70 to 80 percent of money required and the business or owner provides the other 20 to 30 percent. The business or owner's share assures the bank that the owner has money at risk and will be diligent in paying off the loan. The bank normally requires collateral for the amount of the loan. Collateral could be assets like land, buildings or equipment. The owner may be required to sign a personal guarantee for the loan and provide personal collateral for the loan.

Business owners should use the bank staff as advisors and mentors. That's a valuable source of help that's usually free and bank staff have business expertise in many industries.

3-3 Bank Loan Applications

Q. Do you have tips on how to make a successful bank loan application?

A. First, manage your business's credit score with the credit rating agencies. Those agencies collect information from third parties about your debt and credit worthiness performance. Those are things like debt load and payment record. Review the credit reports regularly and make sure they are correct. Submit information about the business that is favorable and will improve the credit rating.

Credit ratings are important. Banks use them to decide whether to approve loan applications. Your customers for large orders or projects use them to determine whether your business is credit worthy to be a reliable supplier. You should use them to decide whether to grant credit terms to your customers.

Second, banks use the 5 C's of credit in reviewing loan applications. Character: Are you known for your word and keep your commitments even when it is difficult to do so? Capacity: Does the business have the capacity to repay the loan as evidenced by the previous 3 years P&L and Balance Sheets and the current year's monthly P&L and Balance Sheet? Collateral: Does the business have equity in buildings, land, and equipment to provide collateral for the face value of the loan? Capital: Does the business's balance sheet show it has total liabilities less than 3 times its assets? Conditions & Common Sense: What are the economic conditions in your industry, market, and the economy? Considering all the factors, does it make sense to approve the loan?

Your loan application package should include a good current business plan, 3 years of financial statements, projected future financial statements, statements of how the loan will be used to improve the business and the legal entity of the business. You also may be asked for an owner's financial statement.

Third, show that you are a good business manager in your business plan and presentation. Show you know how to function in all the roles of a business owner; the Chief Executive Officer (CEO) who does strategic planning and sets goals, the President who executes the plan and goals, the Chief Financial Officer (CFO) who knows financial statements and how to use them to run the business, the Chief Information Technology Officer (CIO) who knows how to use the latest business technology. Also show that you use your advisory team, your banker, accountant, attorney, key suppliers, and key customers to help run the business.

3-4 Getting Start-up Financing

Q. Where can I get start up financing for a business I want to start?

A. Prior to the 2008 financial crisis, startup owners often got bank loans or home equity loans for startup costs. Because of the financial crisis, that's changed because of tighter lending standards and the real estate bust.

As an alternative, more startups are using personal and family savings and credit card debt for startup costs. Online crowd funding is a new potential startup funding source for some kinds of startups.

One survey found that 58 percent of startups 2 years old or younger couldn't get all the financing they needed. Startup cost depends on the industry and nature of the business, but the average for all industries is unchanged at about $50,000. However, recently about 26 percent of the youngest startups started with less than $10,000 compared to 14.2 percent previously. The typical credit card interest rate is more than 15 percent. That's very expensive financing and is only affordable to use for very profitable short-term projects where the balance can be paid off in 1-3 months.

Because of financing difficulty and costs, startups should find every way possible to reduce startup costs. The common ways are:
*Start a home-based business to avoid rent and utility costs.
*Don't sell on credit so current sales revenue is immediately available to pay current expenses.
*Have another source of income for living expenses so the business doesn't have to pay an owner's salary.
*Have an immediate, loyal customer base to produce sales revenue to pay expenses.
*Startup in separate phases or segments to reduce initial cost and make self-funding (bootstrapping) easier.

A business meeting all the above criteria could probably be started with several thousand dollars.

3-5 Sources for Working Capital

Q. Are there sources of working capital financing for small businesses other than bank loans?

A. One new recent source for small business working capital financing is from the small business's large supplier and customers. Many large businesses have idle cash on hand and can borrow at lower rates than their small business suppliers and customers. About 80 of the S&P 500 companies finance their small business suppliers and customers. On the other hand, working capital financing for small businesses from banks has declined since the last recession. Small business loans account for only about 21 percent of bank commercial loans, the lowest in several decades. Small business factoring which is borrowing against outstanding invoices has increased 70 percent.

In some cases, large companies will make loans to small business suppliers in return for a guaranteed multiyear supply of goods at a price indexed to inflation. That provides the large company a reliable supply at a predictable price. Some large companies give suppliers working capital loans.

Some large companies offer suppliers advance payment in return for discounts such as 5 percent for say 2 years. Some large business suppliers will offer customers inventory financing until the product is sold. For example, new car manufacturers typically finance the car dealers' inventory until the vehicle is sold. Large businesses have an advantage over banks in making suppliers and customer loans because they know the business and can assess the risk better and don't have to hold cash reserves for the loans.

Before asking a large business supplier or customer for financing, you should consider what valuable benefit you can offer as an inducement. For a supplier, a guaranteed purchase quantity for a specified period of time with a delivery schedule favorable for the supplier could be a very valuable inducement. Suppliers love predictable sales because it makes their life a lot easier.

Also, offering a predictable purchase price would be a valuable inducement. However, the price should be indexed to some index such as the inflation rate to protect you. For customers, a discount based on payment upon order placement could be a valuable inducement. In my career as a plant manager, we paid our small business maintenance contractor within one week because the contractor didn't have working capital for the usual 30 day pay term.

3-6 Protection against Disasters

Q. How can I protect my small business against disasters?

A. You can't protect your business 100 percent from a major disaster. However, you can protect it well enough to survive and that should be your goal. All businesses need a good disaster preparedness plan to do that. A good disaster preparedness plan has 5 parts.

First, determine your greatest risk potential. Inspect the business's building and evaluate the property damage risk. If you rent your building, the lease probably says the landlord is responsible for building property damage. However, I'll bet it doesn't include your property damage and business interruption risks which could be up to total loss and months of business interruption losses until the building can be repaired and suitable for your operation.

That's your risk and liability. The next major source of damage is roof damage that causes water damage to the building interior and contents. How old is it and what condition is it in? Roofs deteriorate with age. Fires are a major cause of building damage and content damage. Electrical wiring shorts are a major cause of building fires. Does the building wiring pass current codes and is it in good condition?

Second, review your insurance coverage. You need a business owners policy. Consider an independent insurance broker who can shop for the policy with the most coverage and least cost possible. Consider business interruption insurance that covers lost income if the business can't operate. Consider how much you can afford to self-insure with high deductibles to hold costs down.

Third, build a crisis communication plan to communicate with staff, customers, vendors, and contractors during and after a disaster. Consider email and social media. Fourth, protect your vital records. Plan to protect your computers. Have offsite back up files. Scan and backup hard copies.

Fifth, prepare your supply chain contingency plan. Have alternate vendors and contractors if your primaries are disrupted.

3-7 Preparing 5-year Strategic Plan

Q. With the rapid changes in business is a 5-year strategic plan worth the effort to make it?

A. Because of the rapid changes in business a 5-year strategic plan is more worthwhile not less. However, only 63 percent of small businesses have one. The 5-year plan should have several scenarios showing how the business will be affected by each scenario and how the business will react.

First, you need a good description of how the business is doing today. That includes sales revenue, cost of goods sold, each expense line item and profit as shown on the P&L and cash flow statement. Identify trends up or down in those metrics and the cause.

Next, ask yourself where you want the business to be in 5 years. Do you want to just retain your market share and grow as the market grows or do you want to increase your market share? What are your personal life goals for 5 years? Do you want to be working in the business?

After you have your 5-year business goals identified work backward to project the sales revenue, cost of goods sold, expenses and profit metrics that will measure the attainment of those goals. If your goal is to maintain market share, that's fairly easy. Project your sales revenue to keep pace with your industry and market growth rate. Project your cost of goods sold and expenses to keep pace with the anticipated rate of inflation.

If your goal is to increase market share or to increase sales revenue by adding new products or services or to development new products or services, it's much harder. Also, if your goal is to significantly reduce expenses, it's much harder. In those cases the 5 year plan requires an action plan that shows in detail how you will accomplish each goal.

Each action plan must identify the resources required in time, money, labor, attention and follow up. Each action plan must have a schedule with intermediate guideposts to measure results. Each action plan must have a stated measurement of results to measure progress.

Each action plan covers the basics of any project of who, what, when, where, how. The who identifies each employee on the goal team and their duties and responsibilities. Project the metrics for each year that will result from accomplishment of that goal. As you progress through the 5 years, compare your actual metrics to your projections and take corrective action if you are under goal.

Only the owner or manager has the knowledge and experience to prepare the 5-year plan. However, after preparing the action plans and projecting the metrics, your bookkeeping service or accountant can prepare the projected P&L for each year of the plan.

3-8 Selling Shares by Crowd Funding

Q. Can I sell shares in my business through crowd funding?

A. That program was authorized by Congress in 2012 in the Jumpstart our Business Startups Act. The revised Reg A increases the maximum that a business can raise to $50 million from $5 million. Under revised Reg A small investors can invest. Previously, the investor had to be accredited, meaning they had to have an annual income of $200,000 or more or have a net worth of $1 million. That requirement eliminated many potential investors.

Revised Reg A requires the business to file audited financial statements with the SEC and, depending on how much is raised, the business may have to give investors an annual financial statement. The business is not required to file an application with each state in which investors reside.

Although the Reg A rules are simpler than those for an Initial Public Offering (IPO), the process could still cost $50,000 to $100,000. That means the dollar amount raised should be at least several million to be cost effective. That eliminates most early stage startups. It's a possible source of capital for established growth businesses that need capital to continue growing.

There are numerous crowd funding websites that handle the sale of shares online. Pick one that will help you with the SEC document filing and help you comply with SEC regulations. Also, pick one that charges reasonable fees. Fees are usually a percent of the amount raised.

Most small businesses don't have audited annual financial statements because that is costly. If you anticipate raising capital through crowd funding, you will need to start audited financial statements several years in advance. It is very difficult to prepare audited financial statements for prior years.

Managing publicly owned businesses is very different from managing privately owned businesses. Having hundreds of small investors is very different from having a few large investors. Large investors usually understand financial statements and don't require a lot of individual attention. Don't expect small investors to understand financial statements. You probably should consider a quarterly investor newsletter to keep investors informed about the business's activity and progress in nonfinancial terms. Time spent keeping investors informed and happy is well spent and if you don't, you may end up with tens or hundreds of disappointed and irate investors and that would be very time consuming and distracting for you and the business. It helps if the investors really believe in the products or services your business provides.

3-9 Alternative Financing

Q. I have always used bank loans to finance my business's finance needs. What is alternative financing and how could I get it and use it?

A. Traditional bank loans are called asset-based lending. The bank provides the loan secured by the borrower's assets which could be land, buildings, inventory, or machinery. With alternative financing the finance company buys the asset and for a fee allows the client to use it.

The cost of bank loans is usually a lot less than the cost of alternative financing. Alternative financing is an option if the business cannot get a bank loan or in special situations where the potential profit from the financing is high and will easily offset the alternative financing cost.

The common types of alternative financing are equipment leasing, inventory financing, factoring, and purchase order financing. Equipment leasing is quite common for small businesses. It is like an individual leasing a car rather than buying it.

The leasing company owns the equipment and leases it to the business which pays a monthly fee for a fixed term, say 5 years. The business typically must have good credit and have been in business for several years. Some finance companies will buy the business's existing equipment and lease it back to the business.

Businesses lease when they cannot or do not want to tie up large amounts of cash by buying it. The business may fear the equipment will become obsolete before its useful life is used up. The business may only need the equipment for a short-term project. Leases are complex with a lot of conditions. Comparison shop and carefully evaluate the lease terms.

With inventory financing the finance company owns the inventory until sold. Inventory financing is complex and difficult to find for most small businesses. If you have a good relationship with your bank and your inventory is readily re-sellable on the market at full value, the bank might be willing to accept inventory as collateral for a conventional bank loan.

Factoring is a more common form of alternative financing. The finance company is the factor, and it buys the business's accounts receivable at a discount and collects from the business's customer when the term is up in, say, 30 days. The business's customer is notified that their invoice has been factored. The factor's discount fee is usually based on the invoice term. For example, a 10-day invoice might be discounted 1 percent of the invoice face value and 6 percent for a 60-day invoice.

With purchase order financing the finance company buys the business's customer purchase order at a discount and when the product or service is delivered the finance company collects from the customer. Purchase order financing is so complex with so many conditions that it is usually not a good option for small businesses.

3-10 Good Use of Investment Capital

Q. How can I get a better return on new capital investment in my business.

A. The profitability of your business 5 years from now depends on how well you invest your available capital in the business today. If you squander your capital in projects that don't produce profits, your business will be worse off in 5 years.

Most businesses have limited capital. Capital comes from the business's internal accumulated profits. You can borrow capital or sell equity in the business, but both of those have costs. Loans require principal and interest payments. Equity sales usually require payout of dividends to the new owners.

One common use of new capital is to purchase new more efficient and productive equipment. In most industries, the equipment suppliers are continuously developing and producing more efficient equipment. Over time, your equipment becomes obsolete and uncompetitive. If you don't continuously replace and update, your business may become uncompetitive in cost, quality and service. Then you are faced with making a large single purchase of new equipment at inflated prices that your competitors bought years earlier at a lower price. It's very difficult to catch up once your business falls behind. The payback is often in labor cost savings. The new machine produces more with less labor. The greater capacity of the new machine may allow you to fill more orders than you could fill before, thus increasing sales revenue and profit. The new equipment may produce better quality and improve service thus making your business more competitive. Identify the benefit and quantify it in dollars of new profit each year. Calculate a payback by dividing the equipment cost by the annual profit increase to determine the payback in years. Paybacks at 1-3 years are good. Paybacks of 5 years or more mean that project may not be the best use of your capital.

Another common use for new capital is for business growth and expansion. You may need more space, inventory, equipment and employees in your present site or there may be another site in another market where you could reproduce your existing, successful operation. However, be careful and analyze the potential growth carefully.

Rapid business growth is very difficult because your costs go up immediately up front, but your sales revenue growth takes months and sometimes even years. Meanwhile profit plunges and you may have large losses while waiting for sales revenue to pick up. Estimate costs, sales, and profits realistically and make sure you have enough cash or credit to survive until the expansion reaches at least breakeven when revenues cover all costs.

Sometimes marketing can be a use for new capital. However, be sure your marketing plan is based on strategies that have a proven track record of producing new sales revenue from the dollars spent.

3-11 Using Business Credit Cards

Q. The only credit I can get for my small business is a business credit card. Is that safe?

A. It depends on the nature of your business and how you use the credit card. Many lenders don't make small loans because the cost to administer a small loan is high compared to the interest income received. Only about 39 percent of bank loan requests from small businesses are approved. On the other hand, 75 percent of small businesses are successful in obtaining business credit cards. The result is that about 59 percent of small businesses use credit cards to meet their credit needs.

When used right credit cards have numerous advantages. The first 30 days of credit has no interest charges. Purchasing materials, supplies and services with credit cards transfers the credit cost to the supplier. Credit card statements provide documentation of purchases that can be easily posted electronically to the business's books. Credit cards provide credit for large, unexpected expenses until other lower cost credit can be obtained. They are a convenient and time saving way to pay bills.

Many small businesses sell for cash, check or credit card and do not offer term credit to their customers. They often receive credit terms of 15 to 30 days from their suppliers of materials, supplies and services. Their need for working capital to fill the gap between when they receive customer payment and when they pay suppliers is less than 30 days. The credit card provides free credit for 30 days. In effect, they pay current bills with current revenue with the help of a credit card.

Carrying credit card balances past 30 days and paying the high annual interest rate of typically 18 percent is profitable if your profit margin as a percent of sales revenue is high like 15 percent. Let's say it's 90 days after you pay your suppliers before you are paid by your customer for an order. You pay your supplies with the credit card and owe no interest for the first thirty days. You pay the credit card company 1.5 percent interest per month for the 2 months totaling 3 percent. Deduct that 3 percent cost from your 15 percent profit margin and you still make a nice 12 percent profit. That of course doesn't work if your profit margin is 5 percent.

The danger of credit card credit is if you run up a large 30 day plus balance and the business is not producing enough free cash to pay the high monthly interest charges and also quickly pay down the 30 days plus balance. That means the business is in a death spiral with ever increasing debt and interest charges. Avoid that by only running a 30 day plus balance if you are certain, you will have the cash to pay off the 30 days plus balance within 2 to 3 months.

CHAPTER FOUR

BUSINESS MANAGEMENT SKILLS

SUMMARY

- If you assign a task to a subordinate worker without your regular follow up, it will never get done.
-
- If you have 20 subordinate workers and delegate and manage them well, you increase your personal output by 20 times.
-
- Without a goal and action plan to get there, you never accomplish anything.

CHAPTER FOUR
BUSINESS MANAGEMENT SKILLS

4-1 Good Management Techniques	87
4-2 Different Kinds of Managers	89
4-3 Leadership	91
4-4 Management Skills and Techniques	93
4-5 Better Decision Making	95
4-6 Better Planning	97
4-7 Chance and Business Success	99
4-8 Productive Managers	101
4-9 Good Decision Making	103
4-10 Learning from Business Failures	105
4-11 Organize and Delegate	107
4-12 Managing Millennials	109
4-13 Middle Managers	111
4-14 Best Practices for Project Management	113
4-15 Critical Employee Performance	115
4-16 Productive Meetings	117
4-17 Remote Managers	119
4-18 Task Assignment	121

4-1 Good Management Techniques

Q. How important is good management to the success of a business?

A. If you've ever worked for a poorly managed business or a poorly managed department of a large business, it's obvious how important good management is to success. Success is measured by productivity (units of goods or services produced per worker hour), profitability, cost control, growth, and survival.

An ongoing 10-year research project studied the performance of 10,000 businesses in 20 countries. The research focused on the three management techniques: setting targets, rewarding performance, and measuring results. The US had the best managed companies. Large multinational companies got high scores. Government owned and family businesses had the lowest scores.

US businesses are 30 percent more productive than European businesses. Good management in the US companies accounted for a quarter of that 30 percent productivity gap. During the 2007-08 financial crisis and recession US businesses in hard hit industries that practiced the good management techniques of setting targets, rewarding performance, and measuring results did considerably better than those that didn't.

Another survey of more than 30,000 US factories found that those that practiced setting targets, rewarding performance, and measuring results had superior performance compared to those that didn't. Economists say the quality of management depends on how fierce the industry competition is. That's why US businesses and large multinationals are better managed. They face fierce competition. The badly managed businesses fail, and the well managed ones survive and prosper.

The key management techniques are setting targets, rewarding performance, and measuring results. If you don't set targets that determine success, the business is not focused on what counts and doesn't know whether it succeeds or fails. Each target should have an action plan stating how the target will be accomplished, employee responsible and the resources of labor and money required. The action plan should also have intermediate milepost to measure progress and final completion date.

Rewarding performance motivates the work force from top to bottom, however, keep in mind a lot of business success is a team effort not individual effort. Measuring results is critical. Without measuring results, you don't know what works and what doesn't or whether you are succeeding or failing.

Other important management techniques are planning, organization, delegation, decision making, communication, coordination, collaboration, resource allocation, risk control and follow up. Those management techniques become more important as the business grows in number of employees and complexity. Without those management techniques a large complex business degenerates into chaos and nothing gets done. It's amazing how much easier it is for each worker to accomplish their job in a well-managed business compared to a poorly managed one.

4-2 Different Kinds of Managers

Q. Are there different kinds of managers?

A. Yes. There are leaders, managers, and administrators, depending on the size and complexity of the organization. They all use the common management skills of goal setting, and enforcement, of policies and procedures, planning, decision making, organization, delegation, task assignment, follow-up, measurement of results, rewarding performance, and leadership. However, they use those to different degrees.

Leaders manage smaller teams up to about 800 team members. They are usually located onsite with the team members. They interact with the team members face-to-face daily. They know the strengths and weaknesses of the key team members and assign tasks that maximize their strengths and minimize their weaknesses. They expect and receive loyalty from team members based on the team member's personal observation of the leader's professional skills and the leader is loyal to the team members by looking after their welfare as well as possible. The leader sets goals for the team, designs action plans to achieve the goals that clearly define the who, what, when, where and how for each goal. The leader shares in the team's hardships and the recognition when the goals are achieved. A historic example of a good leader was Lewis of the famous Louis and Clarke expedition in the early 1800's to explore the US Northwest. The team had about 30 members and achieved its goal.

Managers lead teams larger than about 800 members. The organization is more complex and usually has numerous sub-goals that are required to achieve its main goal. The team is normally organized in functional departments with each one having its own leader. The usual departments of a business are production, marketing and sales, finance and accounting, human resources, and purchasing. The manager may or may not be located onsite with the team. The manager leads through the department leaders, not directly with team members. The manager issues all action orders through the department leaders and never bypasses them. In my career as a business manager, I welcomed and sought information about the operation directly from team members, but never bypassed my department leaders when issuing action orders. Managers should have the professional skills to inspire loyalty from team members. However, loyalty goes both up and down. The manager should earn that loyalty by looking after the personal welfare of team members. Managers use all the management skills.

Administrators lead very large teams in very complex organizations. Administrators usually have numerous managers reporting to them and lead through those managers. Administrators set goals and issue policy and procedures and enforce them. A good example is the administration of a large hospital. The administrator provides the trained medical staff, equipment and building. However, the medical staff make all the patient care decisions and manage patient care. The administrator has no authority in that area. Another example is governments and agencies. A good historical example of a failed administrator is Lewis of the famous Lewis and Clark expedition. After the successful expedition, President Jefferson appointed Lewis Governor of the Indian Territories he had explored. Lewis did not know how to be an administrator and failed miserably.

4-3 Leadership

Q. How can I be a better leader?
A. Managers function as leaders, managers, or administrators depending on the size and complexity of the organization managed. However, all three use leadership skills. Managers lead their subordinate leaders and administrators lead their subordinate managers.

Leaders must be professionally competent in the job they hold to gain the respect and confidence of subordinates reporting to them. No one can work productively for an incompetent boss. Chaos and disorder results. Leaders must have the loyalty of subordinates who report to them. That loyalty is earned with actions not words. Loyalty is earned by taking care of the subordinate's welfare.

The best example of earned loyalty is General Washington during the American Revolution. Washington's army was withdrawing across a bridge on a cold, wet winter night. His engineers had mined the bridge to blow up when the last soldiers were safely across. As the last soldier came ashore in the dark, he bumped into the leg of a man on a horse. He looked up and recognized Washington. He was there to be sure all his soldiers got safely across. Washington could have been back in his command post in a dry, warm farmhouse or at least in his dry, warm tent. Instead, he was out in the cold, wet weather ensuring his soldiers were safe. Washington had fierce, personal loyalty from his army of thousands of soldiers. He earned it. Leaders share the dangers and hardships of their subordinates.

Leaders set goals for their organization and design action plans to accomplish those goals that spell out the details of who, what, when, where, why and how required. They make assignments to subordinates that maximize their strengths and minimize their weaknesses. They measure results and recognize good performance. They monitor progress and intervene if necessary to keep assignments on schedule. After the goal is accomplished, they perform an after-action review to determine what went well and what did not. They and their subordinates learn from failures and resolve to not repeat those. Good leaders allow the subordinate to decide how to accomplish the task. If the task turns out well, that is a great sense of satisfaction for the subordinate and creates initiative for the next assignment. Good leaders treat their subordinates fairly and have consistent expectations from them. Consistent expectations are necessary for a smooth functioning operation.

4-4 Management Skills and Techniques

Q. What management skills and techniques are most important for a new start up business?

A. One study of about 200 Silicon Valley startups in the 1990s. The study identified 5 types of business management culture and tracked the success of each.

Type #1 they called the "star" model. They hired only elite managers from elite universities or other elite successful companies. They gave the managers a lot of autonomy and lavish perks. Type #2 they called the "engineering" model. They hired engineers with the engineer problem solving mind set. There weren't many "stars" among the engineers. All of them were equal. Type #3 they called the "bureaucracy" model. They had many middle managers with job descriptions, organization charts and employee handbooks. Type #4 they called the "autocracy" model. That was similar to the bureaucracy except everything was dictated by the founder or CEO. Type #5 they called the "commitment" model. They emphasized commitment of management to workers and commitment of workers to the company. They promised long term, including lifetime employment. They only laid off employees if the future of the company was threatened.

The study tracked the companies' performance over 10 years. About half survived 10 years and some became major corporations in their industry. The "star" type produced many highly successful companies, but they also failed in large numbers. Infighting among the key stars often created dissention in the company that hurt its performance. The consistent winner was the "commitment" model. They selected better employees who were more dedicated and productive. They functioned smoother as teams and organizations. They responded to customers better. Employees trusted each other. Employees were well trained. They were loyal and had low turnover.

In my business career, I found good management is more complex than a single model or 5 rules or secrets as some management gurus promote. Good management requires good employee selection, effective assignments, setting expectations, good communication, coordination, follow up, feedback, organization, delegation, motivation, training, planning, decision making and resource allocations.

4-5 Better Decision Making

Q. How can I learn to make better business decisions?

A. In recent years studies of how the brain works to make tough decisions are rebutting long held beliefs about business decision making. The conscious brain can only work on one calculation at time. The unconscious brain can work on billions of calculations at the same time.

Most companies expect decision makers to make good decisions 40 hours each week. When surveyed those decision makers say they are at the peak of their game only 3 to 5 hours each week. Only 10 percent said they did their best thinking at work, but 39 percent said they did their best thinking at home.

Researchers use brain scanning equipment to determine which parts of the brain are active when a test subject is making decisions and the intensity of the activity. Past accepted wisdom was that tight deadlines inspire better decisions. Brain scan studies show the opposite is true. Deadlines limit our thinking and can cause worse decisions. The more stressful the deadline the less open we are to consider other, better options. The part of our brain that performs tasks and solves problems is active but the park of the brain that produces original ideas is not.

We commonly believe that we use the logical part of the brain to make tough decisions, but studies show that the best strategists use more of the emotional, social and intuitive parts of the brain. They go more with their gut feelings rather than entirely with logic. We can't avoid deadlines, but decision makers can learn to reduce stress and intentionally let their minds wander with techniques like meditation that activate the creative part of the brain.

Uncertainty about your job or your business's future can lead to bad decisions. The uncertainty activates the brain centers associated with anxiety and create a doom and gloom attitude. Studies show that 75 percent of businesspeople in uncertain situations wrongly assume bad things will happen. They make wrong decisions to prevent or mitigate bad things that never happen. Recognizing our tendency to exaggerate the problem helps us have a better perspective. Usually, decisions are not final. They can be changed as the situation changes. In my career the worst outcome rarely happened.

The best leaders and decision makers can motivate people with encouragement, praise and rewards. That creates a sense of purpose and a strong emotional bond with the leader. They can inspire others by communicating their vision clearly and getting buy in and commitment.

Researchers are near the point of being able to teach decision makers to rewire their brains through neurofeedback. The objective is to identify the brain patterns that produce better decisions and teach decision makers how to develop those patterns.

4-6 Better Planning

Q. How can I be a better planner for my business?

A. Planning is an essential part of good management. Each project should have an action plan and the business should have an annual plan.

The project plan answers the key questions of what-when-why-where-who-how? The "what" portion of the project action plan describes exactly what is to be accomplished. It could be to increase sales revenue by 20 percent, reduce inventory by 10 percent or reduce costs by 10 percent. "When" is the project schedule and completion date. Every project should have a schedule, otherwise it will never be given the necessary priority to get it done. There are always other goals and projects competing for the business's limited resources of employee time and attention and money. Divide the project into well- defined segments and set a completion date for each segment. State whether segments can be worked on simultaneously or in sequence. When possible, work segments simultaneously because that shortens the project completion date. For large projects, there may be what planners call the "critical path" of segments that must be finished in series to complete the project in the shortest time possible. If so, identify the critical path up front so those segments can be given priority. If it's a long duration project, set intermediate mile post target dates. It's easier to manage smaller shortterm segments rather than the whole project.

"Why" is often overlooked. However, employees need to know why the project is important for the business. "Where" state where the action will take place. It could be in house by employees or outsourced to a consultant. "Who" is critical. The plan must state who is responsible for each task or segment. Several employees may work on a task, but one should be designated responsible. "How" describes how the project will be accomplished. Whenever possible, the how should be left to each employee to decide because that is a strong self-motivator.

The annual plan includes a budget for the business and for each major department. The annual plan also has key goals and objectives for the business and each major department. Each goal should be measured, and progress should be reported monthly or quarterly indicating whether the business or department is on goal, above or below goal. If below goal, the owner or general manager should identify why and take corrective action to get back on goal.

4-7 Chance and Business Success

Q. How much does chance determine business success or failure?

A. In my career I found that chance determined many of my business successes and failures. I'd rather be lucky anytime than smart. When you're lucky it guarantees success but when luck is against you no amount of smarts will produce success. Predicting business success is uncertain for the same reason that long range weather forecasts and stock market forecasts are unreliable. There are countless unpredictable events that determine the end result.

Business success depends on the economy, your industry, and your local market none of which you control. It's unlikely you will have business success when the economy is in recession. The economy depends on things like interest rates, wage rates, inflation rates, GDP growth rate, credit availability, unemployment rates, raw material prices, foreign competition, consumer spending, government spending and business capital spending. The economy will affect all businesses to some degree. Try to evaluate what the economy will do in the next year or two but recognize there is a lot of chance in your conclusion.

Your business success depends a lot on the success of your industry. It's difficult to be successful when your industry is failing. Important considerations are the industry growth rate, changing customer taste, foreign competition and consumer sentiment and industry innovation to produce new products and services. Each industry is impacted to a different degree by economic recessions and booms. During the recent recession the sale of big-ticket luxury items declined more than 20 percent while daily necessity items held up well. Older mature industries grow at about the same rate as the GDP growth rate. Newer industries that are still innovating to produce new products and services grow at a much faster rate than GDP.

Finally, your business success depends on conditions in your local market. Again, local markets are affected to different degrees by economic recessions and booms. The local market will depend on things like the local unemployment rate, wage and income rates, consumer spending as measured by the local sales tax revenue and the level of construction as measured by the number and value of construction permits issued.

Try to reduce your vulnerability to failure caused by chance events. Good information reduces risk and produces better decisions. Get outside opinions from your employees, customers, banker, attorney, accountant and outside consultants. Successful businesspeople usually don't bet the business on a single risk decision. Sometimes you can limit the downside risk. For example, when introducing a new product or service, test market it before committing to full production.

Recognize that chance can't be avoided completely. When chance produces business success, appreciate your good fortune. When chance produces failures, don't feel guilty and agonize over your failure. Put it behind you and move on.

4-8 Productive Managers

Q. How can I improve my productivity as a manager?

A. The trend now is for business managers and owners to do more by doing less. That requires strictly controlling your time spent communicating, avoiding interruptions, and delegating. Many managers feel compelled to know everything about everything by constantly communicating by e-mail, social media, smart phone and attending meetings.

If you analyze it, most of that communication is trivia. It produces no useful information you need to manage your business. Screen your address book and keep only those you need to communicate with for essential direction, information, collaboration, coordination, help, advice, and reporting. Of those remaining, monitor their communication but only respond if you need to. Monitoring communication is not time consuming. Responding is.

Studies show that frequent interruptions reduce a manager's productivity by 40 percent and increase stress. The stress comes from having to keep shifting your attention from task to task. Interruption interferes with your focus and focus is essential for complicated work.

Managers perform complicated mental tasks requiring the use of lots of information they have stored in their brain. Interruptions are like computer glitches; they wipe that information out or distort it. It takes time to replace it. It's a lot more productive to perform a complex task through to completion without interruption. Avoiding interruption takes self-discipline to turn off e-mails, smart phones,and social media.

On the other hand, if you reach a mental block on a task and can't come up with the right solution, walk away. Put it on hold. Give your subconscious mind time to work on it. Our conscious mind can only do one calculation at a time. Our subconscious mind can do many.

One manager can do only one day's work regardless how hard or long they work. With good delegation that manager can multiply their personal output by the number of their subordinates. Hire good subordinates who are capable and willing to take on challenges and work with minimum supervision. Train them well. If you make a mistake and hire the wrong person, replace them. When you assign projects explain the end goal. That keeps them focused and encourages big picture thinking.

Give clear, attainable deadlines with intermediate mileposts if the project is long and complex. Put one subordinate in charge. Work teams without leaders don't work. Don't assign similar tasks to multiple subordinates. That's duplication of effort. Don't micromanage. Monitor progress but don't interfere if the project is progressing on schedule.

Recognize and celebrate project mileposts. Instead of choosing subordinates for a project, describe the project and ask for volunteers. People like to work on projects that use their best skills and create satisfaction. What turns one person on will not appeal to another.

4-9 Good Decision Making

Q. How important is good decision making to a successful business?

A. A lot. There are 8 traits of very successful productive people. Decision making is one of the 8. Decision making requires trying to predict the future. In trying to predict the future, what you know is important, but you also must recognize what you don't know and can't know. There's always a degree of uncertainty about the future. To make decisions you must be able to cope with doubt. Psychologists find the best decision makers think in terms of probabilities, not in terms of right or wrong.

You don't need a degree in statistics to estimate probabilities, but you do need to understand the concept. Think in terms of percentages. In other words, if I do this a hundred times will I be right 70 times or 70 percent of the time? You need to be able to consider conflicting potential outcomes and assign probabilities to each outcome. You choose the one with the highest probability of success and the lowest probability of failure. In some cases, your decision will be wrong, but in the long term your accumulative decisions will be right. Good card gamblers know that if they always make a play with better than 50 percent probability of success, in the long run after 100 plays, they will be successful.

Intuition is also useful in estimating probabilities. For example, if something has worked in most cases in the past, it is likely to have the same probability in the future if conditions stay the same. A person who is 40 years old and in good health probably has a long-life expectancy. Our intuition is based on our life experiences, but our life experiences may be biased. In other words, it's not a representative sample.

In making business decisions, we also must consider the magnitude of a right or wrong outcome. Business risk has two parts; the probability of success or failure and the magnitude of a right or wrong outcome. Never take large risk when the potential benefit is small. However, if the potential benefit is very large, higher risk may sometimes be justified. Never take high risk when the potential damage of failure is catastrophic for you or the business. In other words, never bet the business on one decision or project. Take calculated risk not reckless risk.

4-10 Learning from Business Failures

Q. How can I and my subordinates learn from our business failures?

A. Learning from your failure is a process and as in many things there are right and wrong processes. First, set a good example for your subordinates by acknowledging your own personal failures. That conveys the message that failures are a learning process not a punishment process. You want subordinates to report pending failures as early as possible because that provides an early warning to take action to minimize the consequences. Otherwise, a failure that could be corrected with minimum damage will continue to grow and ultimately cause major damage. Many business processes are trial and error. You try something based on assumptions and limited facts and judgment which may or may not work. If it doesn't work, you want to minimize the damage not fix blame.

Second, when failure occurs ask the right questions. Which are what, where how and why. Don't ask who was responsible. That means you're looking for someone to blame. Failures are an opportunity to build trust.

Third, treat business projects as scientific experiments. Projects are based on assumptions, facts and judgment and the only way to find out if they are correct is to try it in the real world. Scientists expect experiments to fail often and when they do it tells them what does not work. That's valuable knowledge. For example, you may do extensive market research, but you don't know for sure a product or service will sell in a market until you try it.

Fourth, control the outcome of failures. You may not be able to avoid failure regardless of how well you study and research a project in advance. You can control how the failure affects you and your subordinates. You don't want failure to create an atmosphere of fear that stifles willingness to try new ideas and innovation. Don't be afraid to praise subordinates for their effort even if the result was failure.

The best workplaces are based on trust between bosses and subordinates and between subordinates. Trust is built when things don't go well not when they do go well.

Think of failures as resources to be used effectively not as losses to be avoided at all costs. Through failures you learn over time what doesn't work and that can be as valuable as knowing what does work. You paid the price for failure so you might as well try to turn it into a benefit.

4-11 Organize and Delegate

Q. How can I organize and delegate to make my business more productive?

A. Even small businesses need to be organized and to delegate authority, responsibility, and accountability. Most businesses organize by functions. The typical functions are production of the product or service, marketing, finance and accounting and Human Resources (HR). As the business grows in size and complexity, more functions are added. For a small business those functions may report directly to the owner.

However, it's important to recognize that the functions are very different and require different skills to manage. Small business owners often are skilled in all functions except finance and accounting. In that case, the owner needs a good outside accountant that they can trust. Still the owner really needs to at least understand financial statements and be able to manage the cash flow. Cash flow management really can't be outsourced effectively and it's too critical to outsource.
Cash flow management is how you know there's money in the bank or credit available to pay debts when they come due. Otherwise, you are bankrupt.

Define what each function is responsible for, preferably in writing. Have a simple organizational chart showing who each function directly reports to. Larger, more complex business may also have functional reporting responsibilities which show as dotted lines on the organizational chart. Dotted lines mean that worker should coordinate their work with the worker designated but will report directly as shown by the solid line. For larger businesses, functional departments will have their own annual budget goals. Even for small business, it's better if you have functional budgets. That makes it easier to manage and control cost.

Good delegation is the key to efficient operations. Some business owners tend to delegate responsibility and accountability, but not authority. A worker can't be responsible and accountable if they don't have the necessary authority. They are constantly seeking approval from the owner and that causes delays and inefficiencies. To be efficient, authority should be delegated to the lowest level worker who has the required knowledge, experience, and information to make the decision. Authority can be on a conditional basis. For example, workers typically have a higher authority spending level if the item is in the approved budget and a much lower level if it's not in the approved budget.

4-12 Managing Millennials

Q. Does it require a different management style to manage millennials?

A. Millennials are those born between 1990 and 2000 also referred to as generation Y. Millennials are 37 percent of the US workforce compared to 34 percent for baby boomers who are rapidly retiring. Millennials are the first generation to have grown up in the digital age. Human behavior research indicates there are many misconceptions about them. One consulting firm polls 90,000 workers each quarter. Contrary to popular belief, millennials are competitive. Fifty nine percent said competition is what gets them up in the morning compared to 50 percent for baby boomers. Fifty eight percent said they compare themselves to their peers compared to 48 percent for other generations. Millennials spend a lot of time communicating with others by smart phones, but 37 percent said they don't trust their peers' input at work compared to 26 percent for other generations. They are individuals not collaborators as commonly thought.

Contrary to popular thought millennials are careerists. Thirty three percent said future career opportunities was in the top 5 reasons for choosing a job compared to 21 percent for other generations. Contrary to popular thought, only 35 percent emphasized corporate do-goodery compared to 41 percent for baby boomers. It's popularly thought that millennials don't want to be told what to do. However, 41 percent said employees should do what managers tell them to do compared with 30 percent of baby boomers. Millennials use smart phones and social media a lot but 90 percent said they wanted to receive performance feedback face to face.

Millennials are mobile in their career. Fifty one percent said they would look for a job change within one year. Job mobility is the key distinguishing trait about millennials. Previous generations were more reluctant to change jobs. Businesses that want to retain millennials will have to work hard to satisfy their career goals and retain them. Millennials attention spans are shorter. They like short instruction periods followed by practice to apply what they learned.

Millennials want to know why they are told to do things. Millennials also learn better with visual instruction rather than with verbal or written instructions. They want a relationship with their boss and respond to personal attention. They like twoway dialog and an opportunity to share ideas face to face. They are good at multitasking.

Millennials are very different in their activities and behavior, but not very different in the workplace. Contrary to popular thought, they don't require collaboration and business do-goodery. They want individual recognition and reward for good work and clear paths to career advancement. They want interesting work and the chance to work hard and get ahead. That's really no different than previous generations.

4-13 Middle Managers

Q. I recently read an article that said there's no future for business middle managers. I'm a middle manager. Is that right?

A. Based on my 45-year business career I'd say that's wrong. Middle managers are those between first level supervisors who directly supervise workers and top management. Middle managers are the ones who execute the policies, goals and strategies of top management and turn plans into reality. They do the planning, make the decisions, allocate resources of money and labor, communicate, coordinate, collaborate, schedule, monitor progress, expedite, follow up, trouble shoot and solve problems. Workers and first line supervisors cannot perform those duties. They don't have the knowledge, experience, skill, capability, and authority to perform those duties. Most workers and first line supervisors want to work in a business with capable middle managers. Otherwise, chaos results and nothing gets done. Every task becomes much more difficult and time consuming. Bickering and disputes arise that sap morale and productivity.

The need for middle managers depends on the size and complexity of the business. A simple service business with the owner and about 10 to 20 employees wouldn't need a middle manager. The owner would still need to outsource specialty services that middle managers do in a larger business-like advertising, accounting, payroll, human resources, and financial services. As a business grows and complexity, middle managers are needed. The typical organization is a middle manager for each major business function. Typical titles would be managers of marketing, production, finance and accounting and human resources.

If the business produces a technically complex product or service, it may need a manager of engineering. If it produces new products and services to remain competitive and grow, it may need a manager of research and development. If it is subject to many environmental and safety regulations, it may need a manager of environmental, health and safety. If it buys large quantities of raw material, parts and supplies from outside suppliers, it may need a purchasing manager and a logistics manager. The logistics manager ensures that raw materials, parts and supplies are shipped by the lowest cost mode of shipment to still arrive on time. As the business grows very large and complex, still more middle manager titles are needed.

Each of those middle manager titles are technical specialties. It takes years of training and experience to acquire the knowledge and skills required. No one person can become expert in all functions. As the business grows the owner or C.E.O. must learn to delegate. That's a major hurdle for many small business owners whose business grows large. They must back away from day-to-day operations and become planners, goal setters, resource allocators, organizers, delegators, communicators, monitors and follow uppers.

4-14 Best Practices for Project Management

Q. Can you give me best practices for construction project management?

A. The following best practices for managing construction projects are well known to professional construction project managers:

Each project should be identified and have its own separate file to record work scope, original bid cost, reason for all scope changes and cost increases and the actual cost to date. The project owner should have a real time cost tracking system to record all committed cost to date. If the project is overspent, the owner and contractor should determine why and take corrective action. The project size should be tailored to fit the capabilities of the bidding contractors. It is urgent that the project scope be defined as accurately as possible prior to bidding. That requires extensive inspection and engineering in advance. If the company can't do that, it should contract with an engineering company to provide that service. If the project scope is poorly defined, contractors will bid very high or refuse to make guaranteed lump sum bids. Either way, the company will incur extra cost and risk for the project.

Each project should be competitively bid separately on a lump sum basis if possible and the scope of work should be included in the request for bid. The project should be let to the lowest bidder. All bidders should be pre-qualified to ensure the bidder has the financial and operational capability to complete the project. All bidders should be required to submit cost saving measures to be included in the project. Each project must have a written agreement between the contractor and owner. All cost escalation for labor or material inflation must be included in the agreement.

All scope changes due to unexpected work must be covered by a written change order agreement between the contractor and the owner before the change work starts and state the reason for the change and the agreed cost and schedule. If the scope change can't be defined the change order can be done on a time and material basis and the contractor should fully document the time cost for labor and equipment and material cost.

All project delay claims by the contractor caused by the owner must be submitted promptly in writing describing the delay and justifying the delay cost. Delay claims must be approved in writing by the owner prior to payment.

Completed work must be inspected for quality and completion and approved by the owner prior to payment. If the owner doesn't have qualified inspectors, it should hire third party independent inspectors and include that cost in the total project cost.

4-15 Critical Employee Performance

Q. How critical should I be on employee performance reviews?

A. That depends on whether it's a routine, periodic review or a review of an employee whose poor performance is a serious problem. For periodic reviews, companies are tending to emphasize the positive things about the employee rather than the negative. Companies fear critical reviews will damage the employee's confidence and harm productivity and performance rather than helping. Employers tend to give frequent praise and urge employees to celebrate their successes. Reviews concentrate on employee's strengths rather than their weaknesses.

The manager points out how the employee can use their strengths better to improve performance. Some companies have a policy to not point out more than one or two weaknesses. For example: some companies ask employees to suggest ideas for their own improvement rather than review performance.

However, performance appraisal shouldn't be entirely positive. Employees really want a fair critique. They like to know where they stand. Appraisals shouldn't praise employees generally for doing a good job. Employees like to know exactly what they did well and what they didn't do well. It's not just management practices that are getting softer and more positive. The same is taking place in the classroom and elsewhere.

Suggested improvements should focus on things the employee can change. Things like personality traits and manner of speech are very difficult to change.

Reviews shouldn't ignore real problems that will only fester and get worse. Those problems will affect the employee's co-worker productivity and team morale. If one work team member's performance is poor and unreliable, it pulls the entire team down. If the company's policies are too lenient, managers will tend to avoid the employee's weaknesses because it's unpleasant to confront employees.

Problem employees are a special case that should be handled outside the periodic review process. The review should identify specific failures and specify what the employee must do to become a satisfactory employee. Usually, the employee is put on probation for a specific time period to improve their performance and become satisfactory. Additional reviews should be held during the probation to measure the employee's progress and provide feedback.

4-16 Productive Meetings

Q. How can I make business meetings more productive?

A. One business school study indicated managers spend 18 hours a week in meetings. Meetings can serve a useful purpose or be a total waste of time. There are six rules to follow to ensure meeting are productive.

First, have a necessary purpose. In many cases the purpose would be served equally well with an email or phone call.

Second, decide who needs to attend. Keep the number of attendees as small as possible. More people mean more discussion and longer meetings. Include only those who will be affected by any decisions made or who have essential information or skills to contribute to the discussion. Don't include those who only need to know the outcome of the meeting. Those can be informed later by email or phone.

Third, start on time and end on time. Cut off rambling, unnecessary discussion and move on. Some people like to hear themselves talk and love to make suggestions for other people to work on with no intention of doing anything themselves. That can be pre-empted by assigning anyone making a suggestion responsibility for completing it.

Fourth, have an agenda and stick to it.

Fifth, keep it short. Preferable one hour or less and never more than two hours. People become unfocused and unproductive. Don't function as a committee of the whole and try to resolve all details in the meeting. Assign one attendee to research the issue and report back later with an action plan.

Sixth, give attendees time to prepare. Give attendees a meeting outline one or two days in advance so they know what is expected and can come prepared. If the meeting purpose is a new, complex project, attendees may need more notice to properly prepare. In that case, the meeting conductor may need to make specific assignments to attendees to research issues and come prepared to present an action plan.

Meetings should be for purposes that require face to face negotiation, collaboration, feedback and buy in by the attendees. Other topics can usually be handled equally well by email, phone or conference calls. Meetings should end with specific task assignments to attendees to carry out any decision made along with completion and report back dates. Never assign follow up responsibility to all meeting attendees. Each will assume the others will do it and the result is that no one does it. The meeting will have been a waste of time.

4-17 Remote Managers

Q. My manager and I are located in different cities and rarely meet face to face. How can I communicate better with my manager?

A. There are best practices for communicating with your remotely located manager. Try to agree with your manager on what decisions you can make on your own and what decisions your manager will make. That will avoid misunderstanding and confusion. Schedule a regular 20-minute phone call each week to update your manager, report progress and get help or direction on how to proceed. Use a few minutes of the call for personal chatting about personal nonbusiness activities. That helps to establish a personal elationship more like working in the same office.

Match the communication technology to the situation. Email and instant messages are OK for sharing information and ideas. Use video conferencing for brainstorming or planning sessions. Face to face meetings are best for tough decision making requiring collaboration and negotiation or for sensitive topics. If the topic is important, always put it in writing either in email or US mail letter. Human memory is not sufficiently reliable. Two people are likely to remember details differently. Use active listening skills for phone calls and video conferencing by paraphrasing and repeating and questioning to insure you understand each other.

It's harder to build mutual trust remotely and your manager's trust is critical when working remotely. To do that, always deliver on what you promise or promptly explain why you couldn't. Forewarn your manager of any failures or problems you see developing. Managers hate bad surprises. Forewarnings indicate you are in control and on top of the situation. Surprises make the manager wonder what else bad is about to happen and whether you are in control of the situation.

After phone calls on important topics, follow up with an email summarizing what was said and decided. It's too easy to misunderstand verbal conversations.

Report any changes in your plans or significant new events promptly. Remember that your manager reports to higher managers and they all are expected to know about any significant business events. Even if you don't have complete information about the event, report it promptly and follow up with details later.

Try to schedule a face-to-face meeting with your manager every month or two to discuss progress, plans for the future and resolve any glitches in communication. When miscommunication occurs be sure you understand why and take corrective action to prevent recurrence.

It's important that your manager recognize the success and accomplishments of you and your team. That's harder to do remotely. Don't brag or self-promote. State what you did matter-of-factly.

4-18 Task Assignment

Q. How can I make better task assignments to my workers and follow up on their work?

A. There are two types of assignments. The first is repetitive daily tasks and the second is special one-time assignments and tasks. In both cases consider the strengths and weaknesses of the worker. If possible, always assign the task or project to the worker who is strong in that area. Strong means they have good knowledge and skills. That enables you to take advantage of the best capabilities of each worker.

Most tasks and projects are defined by answering the questions, why, who, what, how, when, and where. Workers are more motivated and perform better when they understand why a task or project is important for the business. If the worker is well qualified, you should leave the how for the worker to decide. Human behavior research shows that being able to choose how to do a task is a strong self-motivator and creates job satisfaction. However, if you know something about the task that the worker does not know that would make it easier or better, suggest how to do it.

When means telling the worker the expected completion time or date. If it's a long duration, task, or project, you may want to set intermediate progress deadlines. That makes it easier for you and the worker to keep track of expected progress. Make sure the worker has the tools and materials and information needed to do the task.

Never assign a task or project that you don't intend to follow up on. Workers typically have other tasks and projects underway, and they have to give the new task priority if it's to be done on time. If you don't follow up, the worker will assume it's not important and will give it lowest priority. Lowest priority never gets done. If you don't follow-up to check on progress, the worker may encounter obstacles or problems and be unable to progress without help. They may be delayed waiting for another worker to assist or for material delivery or for necessary information. Don't depend on the worker always reporting when they have delays or problems. You need to be proactive and discuss it. Always encourage workers to report bad news about obstacles and problems. You need to know about problems promptly so you can intervene and solve them before the project is so far behind schedule it cannot catch up. Always be proactive looking for potential delays and problems.

If the task is a routine continuing task, set up a regular monitoring and measuring program management report. If you don't measure a continuing activity, you have no way of knowing how well it's doing.

CHAPTER FIVE

WORKER PRODUCTIVITY

SUMMARY

- Businesspeople should control their smart phone and e-mails, not let it control them.
-
- Allowing the worker to decide how to perform a task is very satisfying and motivating.

CHAPTER 5
WORKER PRODUCTIVITY

5-1 Electronic Communication Impact on Productivity   125
5-2 E-mail and Smart Phone Abuse   127
5-3 Improving Productivity   129
5-4 Motivating worker Productivity   131
5-5 Overuse of Phone in Workplace   133

5-1 Electronic Communication Impact on Productivity

Q. My employees spend a lot of time on mobile communication devices and e-mail that don't seem to help their productivity. Are those devices productive?

A. Worker productivity growth in the US as measured by output per worker per hour has been poor since mobile communication devices and e-mail became popular. Mobile devices include smart phones and tablets. One survey indicated workers receive and send an average of 121 e-mails each workday and spend 45 percent of their work day doing it. It's unknown how much more time they spend on mobile devices doing things other than e-mail.

Before e-mail and mobile devices became popular the average worker spent about 10 percent of their workday communicating. E-mail and mobile devices no doubt help productivity to a degree but when workers spend more than 45 percent of their workday it is questionable whether that is productive. The potential time savings is as much as 35 percent which could be a tremendous boost to productivity.

We humans are social beings. We want to belong to a group, be accepted and appreciated and communicate with the group. We are curious about what others are doing. We want to be continuously in the loop and know what's going on. We are genetically wired that way.

Today's electronic communication makes it so easy; we're over doing it. We are rapidly becoming victims of electronic communication technology rather than users. The providers are more and more in control with things like mobile alerts and users are less and less in control.

It's unlikely workers will have the self-discipline to turn off or limit the use of their devices. Employers will probably need to set policies regarding employee use of those devices. Consider limiting use to business purposes only during work hours except for emergencies.

Define the specific business purposes. Nobody knows how much time workers spend chatting with friends or family, playing games or keeping up with the news. Each business's need for communication will be different considering the type of business and job duties.

Employers may want to consider setting time limits for each employee for an average workday. Mobile device APPs and computer APPs can monitor the time spent and give the employee feedback so that they can better manage their time and alarm when the time is used up.

For some employers or individual employees, it may be desirable to establish periods during the day when they shut down their devices and focus on work. E-mail services have "out of the office" notices and smart phones have voice mail.

Studies have shown that e-mail and phone call interruptions are a major interference with worker productivity. The more complex the work the greater the interference. One study indicated computer programmers lost 10 minutes of productive work for each interruption.

5-2 E-mail and Smart Phone Abuse

Q. Do e-mails and smart phones really improve my business productivity?

A. They do to a degree, but many businesspeople seem to be letting e-mails and smart phones control them rather than using them as productivity tools. One survey indicated US workers receive 11,680 e-mails each year. Fortunately, 74 percent are junk and never reach the worker's in box. That still leaves 3037. Those 3037 consume the equivalent of 111 workdays each year for the average worker. That is about 45 percent of the average worker's work time. For maximum productivity that should not exceed 10 percent for total communication time. That means the average worker is wasting 35 percent of their time.

Many businesspeople seem to think they must be 100 percent informed not only about their work but about everything else going on in the world. Otherwise, they do not feel like a creditable businessperson. That is just not true. They only need to know the important information that affects their work. The remaining e-mail and text messages appeal to the person's curiosity and personal need to be connected, included, and accepted as a member of a group. However, that does not produce business results. In business your time is your most valuable asset. It takes strong self-discipline to use your time wisely to reach your business goals.

E-mail and smart phone "copy" and "reply to all" are greatly overused and interfere with the productivity of the receiver. When you "copy" or "reply to all" to a dozen or more people it sets off a barrage of replies that require several cycles before if finally dies. Only "copy" or "reply to all" to people who really need to know. Do not spend time reading copies and replies that you recognize as a waste of time.

Overuse of e-mails and texts also interfere with prompt decision making. For best productivity, the lowest level person in an organization with the authority, knowledge and experience should make the decision. For large or complex decisions, collaboration and coordination with several others may be necessary but not with dozens of others.

Because e-mail and texting make collaboration and coordination convenient does not mean it is productive. Each person consulted feels compelled to reply with input. That triggers several cycles of responses to reach a resolution which delays the decision and consumes everyone's time that should be used for other productive work. It does not improve the quality of the decision either. Most businesspeople are not likely to curtail e-mail and smart phone use voluntarily. It is just too much fun. Owners and managers need to issue policies and follow up to see that policies are followed.

5-3 Improving Productivity

Q. How can I improve the productivity of my employees?

A. Currently, improving productivity is the best opportunity for most businesses. Since World War II, productivity grew at 2.2 percent per year. In the last 5 years, productivity growth was only 0.5 percent per year. On the other hand, hourly compensation including benefits and health care were up 3.7 percent per year.

If I were active in business, I'd look first at employee online use of computers and cell phones. There's been a number of surveys that showed employees spend a great deal of time surfing online and on social media that is not business related. Businesses need strict policies preventing employee online surfing and social media use during paid business hours. Businesses have always had policies preventing employees from spending excessive time on coffee breaks, socializing and on personal activities. It's high time to control online surfing and social media use.

Businesses should also have policies controlling time spent in meetings and collaboration. Surveys have shown they are great time wasters. There are 5 best practices for conducting efficient meetings. Businesses have greatly over emphasized collaboration. I am amazed at how many people businesses and organizations involve in every project. In many cases, it's a complete waste of the person's time.

Use the old Industrial Engineering Work Simplification process for all operations. It consists of eliminate, combine, separate, change the sequence, reduce and reassign. Some tasks have outlived their usefulness and can be eliminated. Does the task add value? If two workers are doing identical jobs, can one worker do both? If two departments or groups of workers are doing the same work, can one be eliminated by assigning its work to the other? In some cases, the frequency a task is done can be reduced to save labor. Changing the sequence of a task can be more efficient. For example, in assembling products, taking time to fix the problem during assembly is a lot more efficient than tearing the finished product apart and fixing it later.

Sometimes other workers can perform a task more efficiently.

Consider investing in labor saving tools and equipment. In each industry there is labor saving equipment that eliminates manual labor or makes manual labor a lot more productive. It ranges from power hand tools to automatic machines. In many cases the labor cost saving will pay back the tool or equipment cost in 2 to 3 years. You can afford to consider pay backs up to 4 to 5 years. Never assign more than one worker to a task if one worker can physically and safely do the task. Unavoidable interferences make 2 or more worker crews inefficient.

5-4 Motivating worker Productivity

Q. How can I motivate my employees to be more productive?

A. A recent survey of workers attitude toward their work indicates that most businesses have your problem. Unfortunately, you are not alone. The survey classified worker responses in three groups of employees. The first is actively engaged employees which was only 30 percent. Actively engaged meant involved, enthusiastic, committed. That 30 percent equaled the highest response since starting the survey in 2000. The second group is not engaged which was 50 percent. Not engaged meant going through the motions. The third group is actively disengaged which was 20 percent. Disengaged meant they hate their work and actively undermined their employers with their poor attitude.

Those survey results indicate employees are a business's best asset or its worst liability. If you can find a way to motivate the lower 70 percent, you have a gold mine of potential productivity. Part of the poor attitude and productivity no doubt is cultural and it's very difficult to change people after they become adults. However, you can be very selective in hiring and very active in weeding out poor performers. Hire new employees through a temp agency which allows you to evaluate the new hire on the job before hiring them permanently. The temp agency does the recruiting and pre-screening. Based on my career experience by providing competitive wages, benefits and selective hiring and weeding you can improve on the 30-50-20 percentages a lot.

The best motivator is the job itself. Give as much independence, challenging assignments, varied assignments, continuing training, responsibility, and authority as possible. Try to match each employee's strengths, abilities, skills, and interest with the job. Employees like to work in the sweet spot of their talents, skills, and interests. Give as much creative freedom as possible. Creativity applies to any task performed by the mind and hands. Creativity is deeply satisfying. Consider yourself each employee's coach and try to find the key to motivating them. If the employee is well-trained and experienced, allow them to decide how to do each task. That is very motivating when the task is done.

Unfortunately, a lot of work is repetitive, dull and boring by its nature. In repetitive jobs the 50 percent of not engaged workers may still be productive but don't feel good about their work. Help workers find satisfying meaning in their work although repetitive. Emphasize how the product or service makes customer's lives easier and more enjoyable. Encourage a feeling of authorship and ownership. Let employees put their name on the product. Encourage social interaction among employees which satisfies the human desire to be a part of a group. Let employees have input in decisions that affect them. Show your appreciation for good work. Keep employees informed about the business's problems and successes.

5-5 Overuse of Phone in Workplace

Q. How serious is overuse of smart phones by workers during business hours and how can I reduce it?

A. There have been frequent articles in Business Journals indicating overuse of smart phones by workers during business hours is a major problem causing poor productivity. One survey showed the average person spent 2 hours and 25 minutes per day on smart phones. Much of that time was during work hours. Another survey of 2,000 executives and HR managers found overuse of smart phones was a leading productivity killer. Another study found that even the presence of a personal smart phone on the desk reduced the cognitive ability of the worker compared to having the phone stored away.

Businesses have established various rules to control smart phone use.
- A frequent rule is no smart phones, watches, or laptops on during meetings. They find that multitasking is a myth. Workers can't really hear and understand what's said while fiddling with their devices. One manager went as far as threatening to fire workers who brought such devices to meetings.
- Some have rules that if a worker's phone goes off in a meeting that person has to stand for the remainder of the meeting.
- Some ban managers from using cell phones while walking halls or other public spaces. They want managers to establish eye contact and say hello to workers.
- Some require workers to go to a designated area to use cell phones. That's similar to having designated smoking areas in the workplace.
- Some require phone apps on cell phones that measure and record time spent each work day on smart phones and require workers to discipline themselves to not exceed established limits. One manager required those times be posted on a public white board for all to see to shame those spending too much time on cell phones.

Expect some push back from workers when you set rules on use. Workers tend to consider personal cellphone use as a personal right that managers should not control. They will argue they need to stay in touch with family members for personal reasons. They will also argue cell phones help their productivity rather than hurt it. Probably the reality is most of the time is spent playing games or surfing the internet for entertainment which contributes nothing to work.

CHAPTER SIX

STARTING A NEW BUSINESS

SUMMARY

- Perseverance beats brilliance every time.

- Old entrepreneurs are better than young ones.

- Owners must spend their personal time on what produces the best profit-marketing and sales.

CHAPTER 6
STARTING A NEW BUSINESS

6-1 Starting a New Business	137
6-2 Starting a Business	139
6-3 Entrepreneur's Profile	141
6-4 Entrepreneur Courses and Degrees	143
6-5 Focus on Business Startup	145
6-6 How Satisfying it is to Own a Business	147
6-7 New Businesses that Grow Rapidly	149
6-8 Priority at Startup	151
6-9 Shoestring Business Startup	153
6-10 What Makes Entrepreneur Success	155
6-11 Why Businesses Fail	157
6-12 Business Advice	159
6-13 Chances for Success in New Business	161
6-14 Starting a Business at 45	162

6-1 Starting a New Business

Q. What key advice would you give me for starting a new business?

A. I'll answer that with the key wisdom bullet points I've learned by working with more than 300 startup clients. First, try to start a home based business if possible. That eliminates the fixed costs for rent and utilities which have to be paid every month regardless of sales revenue. Second, don't be dependent on the business for your living expenses during the start up. Pension income or a working spouse will accomplish that. Third, never, ever, co-mingle the business's money with your personal or household money. If you do, you'll never know whether the business is profitable. Have a separate business checking account and deposit all revenue in it. Pay all expenses out of it. Your monthly statement will provide all the documentation you need of the business's revenue and expenses.

Fourth, pay yourself an owner's salary from the business checking account. Your business is not profitable until it can pay you a reasonable salary and pay out a profit at the end of the year. Otherwise, you are just selling your personal labor and that's not a business. Fifth, work for a business in that industry and market and establish a personal, loyal customer base who will follow you when you start your business. That will provide immediate, reliable sales revenue to pay your business expenses.

Sixth, as soon as possible, reach the point where two thirds of your customers are repeat customers, and two thirds of your new customers are referred by the repeat customers. Design your marketing program to do that emphasizing customer loyalty. That provides a reliable source of sales revenue. Seventh, don't sell on credit. Sell only for cash, check, debit, or credit card. That eliminates the need for a lot of working capital for accounts receivable and the time and difficulty collecting. Current sales revenue is immediately available to pay current expenses which is a huge benefit.

Eighth, manage your cash constantly and carefully. Make sure monthly revenue is sufficient to pay monthly expenses. If it's not, you have to identify the problem and fix it. Be sure you have enough cash in the bank or in available credit to cover unexpected expenses or large intermittent expenses like insurance premiums.

Ninth, always pay your payroll taxes and state sales taxes on time. Otherwise, the IRS or State will shut you down. Tenth, have 20-30 percent of your startup costs in cash. If you have good collateral, you probably can borrow the remainder. Eleventh, you never know whether customers will buy your product or service until you try it. Test market it as quickly and at the least cost possible.

6-2 Starting a Business

1. Write a business plan. The marketing plan is most important because without customer sales you fail. The finance plan is second most important. Startup cost includes business equipment and tools, initial inventory, lease hold improvements and working capital to cover your losses until the business reaches breakeven. To estimate losses, prepare a pencil or Excel cash flow spread sheet with 12 columns, one for each month. The first row is estimated monthly revenue. Estimate the number of widgets sold times the price. Be realistic. Next row is cost of gods sold (COG). If you buy widgets and resell them, your purchase cost goes there. If you buy raw materials to produce the widgets, the costs go there. Use a row for each expense, such as rent, labor, utilities, owners' salary. Monthly revenue minus COG minus expenses equals profit or loss. Expect a loss for 4-6 months. Add up the losses and that's the working capital you need in cash or credit before you start. Otherwise, you run out of cash before you break even and fail. Don't take a salary if possible until the business can afford it.

2. You decide whether you need business liability insurance. If you think the business might be sued by a customer claiming bad quality work, contact an insurance broker and ask how much a business liability insurance policy will cost. I suggest no more than $50,000 to keep your cost down. Take just enough so the insurance company will pay your legal costs.

3. You need to register the business. I suggest registering as a Sole Proprietorship or LLC. To register a sole proprietorship, go to the county clerk's office in the county you will be doing business in and file a "Doing Business As" (DBA) application giving the business a name. Google and check the phone book to ensure that name is not already being used. To register as a Limited Liability Company (LLC) Google the Texas State Secretary or the Secretary of your state website. Look for the application and instructions. Fill out the application according to the instructions and mail it with a check for the application fee to the State Secretary. The LLC allows you to do business anywhere in your state or any other state.

4. If you don't have enough savings to start up, take your business plan to a bank and make a loan application. The bank will expect you to put up 20-30% of the startup costs and it will lend the remainder, but only if you have good collateral to guarantee the loan. The bank will want equity in land or buildings as collateral or in some cases, a lien on business equipment that has good market resale value. If the bank asks for an SBA loan

guarantee, go to the SBA staff and ask about the SBA loan guarantee program.

5.   Even though you may not have employees, go on the IRS website and apply for an "Employee Identification Number" (EIN). You will have to pay both the employee and employer social security, Medicare and Income Tax quarterly on the salaries you pay yourself for working for the business and the IRS records those taxes by your EIN. IRS accepts either Social Security or EIN depending on business type.

6.   After you have the business registered, set up a business checking account for the business only. Deposit all business revenue into that account and pay all business expenses from that account, including owner salaries and profit. Never mix your personal money with the business's money. That way the bank monthly statements and year end statements will document the business revenue, expense and profit for tax purposes.

7.   Hire a good bookkeeping service to set up the business's books. They should prepare the businesses quarterly IRS Form 941 where you report and pay your owner's social security and Medicare taxes and Federal Income Tax. Also, the bookkeeper should prepare Schedule C to your personal 1040 tax return at the end of the calendar year which reports the business's annual revenue, expenses and profit or loss. You have to pay out all profit to the owner at the end of each year. The profit or loss from Schedule C you will enter on your personal 1040 and pay the tax or deduct the loss. At the end of each year, have the bookkeeper prepare IRS Form 1099 to each supplier you spend more than $600 with and send it to the supplier and IRS.

8.   If State Sales Tax is levied on your sales, you must collect it and pay it quarterly to the State Comptroller office. If you don't, they will shut you down and sue you for the sales tax.

The above are key steps in starting a business.

6-3 Entrepreneur's Profile

Q. I'd like to be an entrepreneur and start my own business. Can you give me a profile of a typical entrepreneur?

A. We usually think of entrepreneurs as being young, high-risk takers. Not true. The average age is 40. That relates to three other characteristics. Seventy percent used their own savings as the main source of startup funding. Seventy percent were married when they launched their first business. Sixty percent had at least one child. Getting married, establishing a household, buying a home and having a first child all take a lot of money. It's not surprising the average age is 40 before the entrepreneur has been able to save enough to start a business. They probably had the desire earlier but not the funds needed to start a business. Startup costs can vary from several thousand dollars for a simple, home-based, self-employed service business to more than one million dollars for a fast-food franchise. Lenders typically require the owner to put in 20 percent cash and hard collateral for the remainder of the loan. Most entrepreneurs don't have that many assets before age 40.

Entrepreneurs usually spend the years between school and age 40 working for someone else. They learn their industry and make their early mistakes at someone else's expense which is smart. They gain in depth experience and management and business skills that are invaluable in starting and running a business.

Entrepreneurs are typically highly educated. Ninety five percent have bachelor's degrees or higher and forty seven percent have advanced degrees. No doubt the highly educated tend to be self-employed professionals like doctors, lawyers and accountants, consultants, and independent contractors. There are 20 million self-employed workers in the US and about 7 million small businesses with employees. I find my entrepreneur clients to be more likely high school graduates and community college graduates starting nonprofessional businesses like retail and service businesses.

Seventy one percent come from middle class backgrounds and less than one percent from extremely wealthy or extremely poor backgrounds. Entrepreneurs tend to come from large families. On average they have 3 siblings. Forty two percent were first born, and fifty two percent were first in the family to start a business. Seventy three percent think luck was an important factor in the success of their business. We normally think being smart, making good decisions and working hard determines business success. In my career I found most of the factors that determined my business success were beyond my control. Chance events determined about 50 percent of my business success. That's probably the reason entrepreneurs often fail at least once before being successful. Persistence is probably the most important characteristic of successful entrepreneurs.

6-4 Entrepreneur Courses and Degrees

Q. A lot of universities offer courses and degrees in entrepreneurship. Are they worthwhile if I want to start a business?

A. There are thousands of universities, community colleges and even high schools offering courses or degrees in entrepreneurship. However, there's no objective measure to prove students benefit and become successful entrepreneurs as a direct result. Entrepreneurship is a current hot business buzz word. There's no agreement on what the content of such courses should be. Despite the lack of proven results there are 1957 full time professors of entrepreneurship.

There's no standard accepted definition of what an entrepreneur is. An entrepreneur degree doesn't qualify a person for specific jobs in business. It's commonly believed that entrepreneurs are young, single, start a high-tech business in Silicon Valley and raise a lot of initial capital.

The truth is the typical entrepreneur is age 40, married, has children, uses their savings for initial capital and start their non-high-tech businesses in places like Montana, Vermont, and Nevada. The Webster Dictionary definition of entrepreneur is "one who assumes the risk and management of a business".

Based on working with more than 350 clients including about 70 percent startups, I question whether entrepreneurship can be taught. Certainly, it can't be taught until everyone agrees on a definition and course content and a way to measure results in the real world not on the campus. Successful entrepreneurship is at least 50 percent chance and that can't be taught in courses. Entrepreneurship is more a matter of personal characteristics like risk taking, adaptability, innovativeness and accepting challenges rather than a defined body of information in a course or degree.

Entrepreneurship is partly innate in our character and partly learned through events and experiences. That's probably why the typical entrepreneur is age 40 and has worked for someone else for more than

15 years. After working with so many startups, I can teach a client how to start and run a business in 2 hours. But that's not entrepreneurship.

Some clients become entrepreneurs, but most don't. Those that don't, start successful, simple businesses that don't require a great deal of risk taking, innovativeness and creativity. They don't create new products and services or improve existing products and services to gain a competitive advantage.

Based on my experience with startups, it's impossible to tell who will succeed and who will fail in advance. It is possible to tell who is more likely to succeed based on their knowledge of how to produce the product or service and business functions like marketing and financial management and have management skills like planning, organizing, goal setting and measuring results and have unique competitive advantages like already knowing their customers.

Most entrepreneurs are not recognized as entrepreneurs until their success proves them to be. Success may be the only true test of entrepreneurship.

6-5 Focus on Business Startup

Q. I'm starting a new business and have trouble avoiding distractions and staying focused on what's important. Do you have any tips for me?

A. You must keep both the business focused and yourself focused. Your business plan must focus intensely on cash flow including revenue, cost of goods sold and expenses for each month of the first 12 months. Project cash flow for the second and third years, however your attention must be totally focused on the first 12 months. Otherwise, the business may fail before you reach year two or three and it won't matter. Don't try to grow to fast or diversify into other lines of business during the first three years. Your personal time, staff, capital, and business know how are limited during start up and can't cope with rapid growth or business diversification.

I have had clients who have wonderful visions for their new business in 5 or 10 years. They fill their business plan with details about what the business will be achieving in the long term and neglect to show how the business will break even in the first 6 to 12 months. Visions are great but the business plan must have specific measurable goals for each month and each year, action plans to accomplish those goals and most important great execution of the action plans to accomplish those goals. Execution takes focus, dedication, perseverance and follow up. Finally, you must measure results, otherwise you don't know whether the goals were accomplished.

Personal focus is essential to accomplish both short term or long term tasks. Short term tasks may take a few minutes or many hours. You must be able to close your mind to all distractions and focus on the task at hand whether it be making a sale to a customer, balancing the books, or making a presentation to your banker for a loan. Don't try to multitask when doing short term tasks. Give it all your attention.

Focusing on long term tasks is like a juggler keeping 8 balls in the air. Multitasking is essential to keep several dozen ongoing projects progressing on schedule. I have known people in business who absolutely could not multitask. Give them one project at a time and they were great. Give them multiple projects and nothing got done. Unfortunately, in business most projects can't be completed in one sitting. They stretch over days, weeks, and months. You need a suspense file system to keep track of the status of each project and the next date it will need your attention. Computers and electronic communication devices have programs. A simple 12-month desk or pocket calendar works just as well. List the project or task on the calendar on the dates it will need your follow up. When that date arrives review the project status and do whatever is needed to advance it.

6-6 How Satisfying it is to Own a Business

Q. How satisfying is it to own your own business?

A. It's commonly thought that more money and independence are the primary satisfactions of owning your own business. Research in psychology indicates those are important, but not sufficient in themselves. Money can be disappointing if the entrepreneur feels that based on their education in an elite school and previous experiences entitle them to more money. Independence and professional freedom free the owner of bureaucracy and provides the opportunity to decide what they will do and how and when they do it.

Freedom allows the owner to be more creative without being overruled by bosses and that's very satisfying. However, bosses and bureaucracies do provide checks and balances to prevent the business from adopting bad ideas. An owner doesn't have those checks and balances that require them to justify their ideas. That could be dangerous. However, when you own a business, the customer is your boss and may be more demanding and ruthless than any large business bureaucracy. In a competitive business, there's no such thing as complete freedom.

Other key factors to satisfaction are variety of work done, doing tasks from start to finish and seeing identifiable results and getting feedback on their performance. Those factors are more important to entrepreneurs than for managers of large businesses. They gain greater satisfaction from them. An entrepreneur can have greater variety by adding tasks to the business. That could be adding new products or services, entering new markets, targeting new customers, or growing the business which is always challenging. It's key for the entrepreneur to stay with their skill set and core competency.

Getting feedback is especially difficult for entrepreneurs because they typically work alone. They can provide their own feedback by breaking their job into small identifiable tasks rather than broad tasks like improving profitability or sales. With small tasks it's easier to evaluate your performance. Advisory boards and mentors can provide feedback.

Entrepreneur satisfaction also depends on whether they start the business to exploit an opportunity or because of necessity. Opportunity creates more satisfaction than necessity. Also, satisfaction declines with the age of the business. Initially satisfaction is high. Over time the hard work, problems and challenges erode satisfaction. It's commonly thought that inspiration creates business success and satisfaction. Inspiration is constantly eroded by the daily challenges. What matters is dedication, self-discipline and persistence.

6-7 New Businesses that Grow Rapidly

Q. If I start a new business, is it likely to grow rapidly and make me wealthy?

A. There's a misconception that most new small businesses grow rapidly, create most of our new jobs and make the owners wealthy. However, that's only true for about 6 percent of new small businesses. One study indicated that just 6.3 percent of US businesses, mostly small businesses, created all net new jobs between 1994 and 2008. Each of those businesses had annual revenue growth of 25 percent or greater. Annual compounding of revenue is the key. When revenue grows at 25 percent it about doubles every 4 years and quadruples every 8 years. Net profit is likely to grow at the same rate as revenue. Investors and owners who want to become wealthy look for fast growing businesses.

On the other hand, 2 out of 3 new small businesses will not grow big. About 75 percent of new small business owners don't want to grow big. Instead, they are satisfied being their own boss, doing something they like, being able to control their own destiny and have a livable income. The average annual income of US small business owners is about $72,000. Of the 27 million US small businesses about 20 million are self-employed workers without employees. It's not easy to become wealthy just on your own earning ability.

To select a fast-growing business, look for a new fast-growing industry or an industry that's undergoing rapid growth from new technology, new products or services or a change in customers tastes. The radio industry was old and shrinking until about 20 years ago when customer's tastes turned back to radio. Also, pick a local market that's growing rapidly. When the industry or local market is growing rapidly it's a lot easier for you to grow. When your industry or market is growing slowly you can only grow faster by taking market share from competitors. That's hard to do.

Have a new unique product or service that fills an unfilled customer need. Preferably, one that can be protected as intellectual property so competitors can't copy it. Have a product or service that can be easily scaled up from a single local stand-alone business to many other locations by franchising or licensing. Try to anticipate future customer needs and desires and develop products or services to fill the need. Social media companies anticipated people's desire to be in constant communication.

6-8 Priority at Startup

Q. My new small business is about to open its doors. What are the priority things I should spend my personal time on?

A. Owners of startup small businesses should spend their personal time on marketing and sales and financial management. Unfortunately, many owners of startups don't do that, and they fail. I am amazed that many of my start-up clients just assume that customers will find them and buy their product or service without any effort on their part. I had one client who chose the product he would make and sell because he would like to make that product. He gave no thought to whether customers would need and want the product and if so, at what price or how he would get his message out to potential customers.

Marketing is how you find your potential customers and induce them to come in your door or on your website or social media page. Sales is how you induce them to buy once there. The two are very different and require very different strategies and skills. If you dislike marketing and sales, you shouldn't start a new business. Initially, you can't afford to hire expert marketing and sales staff. It's up to you.

The second but equal priority is financial management, especially cash flow management. Hire a good bookkeeping service to produce a monthly cash flow statement that shows the cash receipts and itemized disbursements for each month as well as cash on hand at the start and ending of each month. Don't rely on the bookkeeping service to manage your cash flow. They can't do that. That's your job.

To be sure you have the personal time to market, sell and manage the cash flow, you outsource all you can and delegate the others to your workers. Outsource functions like bookkeeping, Human Resources (recruiting, hiring, payroll and employment taxes). Consider hiring your workers through a temporary agency. They will take care of all that for actual pass-through costs like salaries plus a reasonable fee for their fixed cost and profit.

If you don't know how to market, hire a good marketing consultant to teach you how. However, you must do the marketing because you represent your business, not the consultant.

Owners of new start-up businesses must discipline themselves not to get bogged down in the daily chores of their business and neglect marketing, sales, and cash flow management. If they do, sales revenue drops, their expenses continue, and they run out of cash and fail.

6-9 Shoestring Business Startup

Q.   I recently read a business journal article about starting a business on a shoestring. I'd like to start a business. Is it possible to do it for several hundred dollars?

A.   Yes. It's possible to start a business with several hundred dollars but there are conditions. You need either a day job or a spouse to support you until the business becomes successful. It requires sweat equity in the form of a lot of time and hard work. Avoid high-cost industries. On average it takes about $65,000 to start a business. However, cost can be as high as $82,000 for a construction business, $98,000 for a retail store and $175,000 for a manufacturing business. Instead, you need to choose a home-based business in something like product distribution to retail stores or a service business where you are selling your personal skilled service. Those allow you to bootstrap and pay current expenses from current revenue without a lot of startup capital or working capital.

Technology levels the competitive playing field between large and small businesses and startups VS existing businesses. Make maximum use of tools like interactive websites to market, automated phone-answering systems, social media marketing and E-mail marketing. They give you the capability to reach mass markets inexpensively and conduct real time marketing research to test out new ideas.

A good example would be a computer software and hardware service business for a person skilled in that area. It can be a home-based business eliminating the expense of a costly storefront or shop. There's very few tools and equipment required. There's no inventory. You buy software on the internet or hardware from local stores when the customer needs it. You make a markup profit on the software and hardware. There's a continuing demand for computer service because software and hardware are continuously getting more complex, and most users don't have the technical skills to keep up.

Advertising and marketing are inexpensive.   Effective, low-cost advertising includes business websites, flyers delivered door to door in the target market area, ads in weekly and biweekly neighborhood newspapers for residential customers and in chambers of commerce and business association newsletters for business customers. As you become known word of mouth referrals by satisfied customers is a good source. The only significant other expense is vehicle cost for gasoline and vehicle maintenance. It's a self-employed business, therefore, there's no payroll cost. Total expenses would be about 10 percent of revenue leaving 90 percent of revenue as profit.

Startup cost would be less than $1,000 for initial marketing and advertising. Other current expenses are directly connected to current sales revenue and are paid from current revenue eliminating need for working capital. Therefore, the owner has little start up risk except for their personal time and work.

6-10 What Makes Entrepreneur Success

Q. I've had several entrepreneur business startup failures. Is it time to give up and work for someone else?

A. New Entrepreneurs often fail many times until they get it right and succeed. First, here are tips for entrepreneurs not to do. Don't try to follow examples of successful entrepreneurs. Your situation is never exactly like theirs. Don't read biographies of successful entrepreneurs. The author never has access to how the entrepreneur really succeeded. Don't take the advice of entrepreneurs who say following their passion was the key to their success. Passion results from success. It doesn't create success. Passion doesn't have staying power. It's easy to be passionate when an idea or concept is working well. When things turn bad as they often do in business, passion fades quickly. What creates business success is determination and persistence. As a petroleum refinery plant manager, I had one successful manager reporting to me who was the most determined, persistent businessperson I've known. He was successful because he wore every obstacle out with his persistence.

Don't have careers goals. Instead, have a career system. When you get a new job, immediately start looking for a better job either within your company or outside your company. Don't wait until you need a new job. The probability is that when you need a job the best job won't be available. Setting goals means that you are short of the goal most of the time and feel like a failure. Create something the public wants and be able to reproduce it in large quantities. Having a career system, you learn from each failure and are better prepared for the next venture.

Some of the lessons you will learn are as follows. Good ideas have no value because the world is full of good ideas. What counts is successful execution, not great business ideas or concepts. Choose business ideas and concepts that you can execute. From each venture, learn everything you can about business functions like marketing, advertising, planning, accounting, financial management, financial feasibility analysis, human resources, and management skills. When you do fail, fail forward not backward. That means after each failure you have more knowledge and skills that advance you toward your ultimate goal. Use luck to your advantage. About 50 percent of business success is luck not skill, knowledge, and hard work. However, for luck to work for you, you must be in the game meaning you must be in business for yourself not sitting safely on the side lines by working for someone else.

6-11 Why Businesses Fail

Q. What causes businesses to fail?

A. One study of why publicly traded companies fail identified 6 criteria that determine long term success or failure. The average age of publicly traded companies was 31.6 years, down from about 55 years in 1970. A simplified version of the 5 criteria would apply also to small businesses. The reason for increased failure was first, a harsher less predictable business environment; second, more rapid change due to technological innovation; third, businesses are more interconnected than ever before.

Businesses operate in complex adaptive systems often nested in broader systems. Small businesses have suppliers, employees and customers and operate in a group of competitive businesses and within a larger system including the community and government entities. Businesses can't control what goes on outside the business but must monitor and adapt to survive.

The first criterion is heterogeneity. meaning a diversity of employees, ideas, innovations, and endeavors that help the business adapt to the changing environment. The business must encourage employees to take calculated risk and create new ideas. Learning results from failure.

The second criterion is modularity. Separate modules could be separate business sites in separate markets each operating autonomously. For a retailer that could mean having multiple lines of merchandise not just one. Failure in one wouldn't cause failure in others.

The third criterion is redundancy. For a small business that could mean cross training employees to fill key critical positions. Loss of one key employee wouldn't cause a business failure. Redundancy means having multiple suppliers and customers so that the business can survive loss of one or two. Redundancy could result in less efficiency but could save the business.

The fourth criterion is managers should expect surprises and try to reduce uncertainty. Managers can't predict future changes in the business environment, but they should collect signals, information, intelligence and look for change patterns. When change is identified prepare contingency plans to cope with it or to mitigate the consequences. A new competitor in the market doing things differently should be a red flag signaling change.

The fifth criterion is to create feedback loops and adaptive mechanisms when changes are identified. The feedback should trigger ways to adapt to change.

The sixth criterion is to foster trust and reciprocity with the system of suppliers, customers, competitors, community, and government that the business operates in. Cooperation with those entities is beneficial, but those entities often have opposite interests. Therefore, cooperation requires building trust.

6-12 Business Advice

Q. How can I find good advice for running my business?

A. There are 3 kinds of business advice. First, are best industry practices. That includes how to produce your product or service along with competitive base line measurements like worker productivity and sales per square foot of sales space. That information is typically only available through your industry trade association. Each year association business members voluntarily submit their information in a standard format which the trade association keeps confidential. The association compiles the data and issues the measures in 5 quartiles from the best 20 percent to the worst 20 percent. The association will indicate which quartile your business falls in for each measure. That tells you how your business compares to the competition and what areas you need to work on to improve. Many associations also publish best industry practices for each task in the business. Those best practices are developed by standing committees of association members. Volunteer to serve on those committees. It is a great opportunity to learn the newest cutting-edge practices in your industry.

Second is advice about the business functions including marketing, advertising, accounting, taxes, insurance, financial management, human resources, safety, and training. Each of those functions are different. Seek advisors who are experts in that function with a lot of hands-on experience. A lot of good information and advice is now available online at federal and state agency websites. A few large companies who sell goods and services to small businesses have websites that provide good information and advice to small business owners. Consultants are available on a fee basis, however select the consultant carefully to insure they are really experts in that function. Good consultants can be an asset. Poor ones are worthless. You do not have the time or probably the capability to become expert in all the business functions. Your time should be spent producing the product or service and running the business.

The third kind of business advice is business wisdom. It is the most valuable of all. Wisdom is things like knowing when in the business cycle to expand and take risks and when to hunker down, conserve cash and prepare to survive hard times. You will not find wisdom from consultants. In seeking advice, the trick is knowing how to choose the advisor whether it be a volunteer mentor or a consultant. Pick a person with a lot of successful experience preferably in your industry. They should have good judgment and no conflicts of interest. If your advisor is a volunteer mentor, always express your appreciation for the time and work they spend helping you. That is the only payback they expect.

6-13 Chances for Success in New Business

Q. What are the chances for success for a new business start-up.?
A. About half of new business startups fail within the first five years. However, getting initial help and advice from mentors improves the chances for success considerably. The most difficult obstacles for a new business are getting customers, sales, and marketing. It takes a new business a long time to build up a repeat customer base.

In my business experience, business success is about 50 percent chance, 40 percent skill and dedication of the owner and key employees and about 10 percent innovation. With that said, you can improve on the 50 percent chance of success. First, don't start your business when the economy or your industry are in recession. That helps your chance for success considerably.
Second, start your business when the economy, your industry or your local market are growing. If the local economy grows, all businesses will benefit.

Start your business when interest rates are low. Start-ups need a lot of capital for equipment, tools, inventory and working capital for operating and maintenance expenses until they reach break-even and have enough sales to produce their own working capital internally. Interest rates have been at 40-year lows but are increasing. Low interest rates improve the chances for success. Getting start-up capital and the cost of start-up capital are major obstacles for start-ups.

6-14 Starting a Business at 45

Q. At age 45, am I too old to start a successful business?

A. No. The popular image of highly successful entrepreneurs as being young college dropouts or new college graduates is wrong. A new research paper confirms that fact. The study used Census Bureau data showing the growth of all non-farm businesses with at least one employee plus IRS data for passthrough businesses such as S Corps and LLCs.

Based on all startups in the US over time, the average age of the startup founders was 41.9 years. When the study focused on the most highly successful startups, which is only 0.1 percent of the total startups, the average age of the founders was even higher at 45 years old.

The study also found that the chance for startup success increased steadily with older founders. Founders age 50 plus were about twice as successful as founders in their 30s. Founders in their 20s were least likely to succeed. Age and experience are clearly more important for startup success than youthful energy and disruptive disregard for the status quo.

The 3 most important qualifications for startup success are:
- Deep experience in the industry
- Access to startup financing
- Managerial experience and social maturity

Older founders have gained their industry experience and made the learning mistakes that all professionals make while working for someone else. When they start their own business, they are at the top of their game and make fewer mistakes.

Older founders have accumulated more personal savings which is the primary startup financing. Lenders such as banks are reluctant to lend to startups because they know the failure rate is high and the lending risk is high.

Managerial skill can't be taught by business schools. It must be learned by actual hands-on experience. Older founders get that skill and make their learning mistakes while working for other businesses. When they start their own business, they are at the top of their game as managers and make fewer mistakes.

At age 45 you are at the perfect age to start a successful business.

CHAPTER SEVEN

HIRING AND TRAINING

SUMMARY

- Regardless how thoroughly you interview applicates, you never know if they fit the job until you try them.
-
- Older candidates are usually better candidates.
-
- Expect to train new workers for the job. It is unrealistic to expect them to start to work on day #1.

CHAPTER 7
HIRING AND TRAINING

7-1 Hiring and Training	166
7-2 Channels for Hiring	168
7-3 Finding Qualified Employees	170
7-4 Hiring New Employees	172
7-5 Hiring Older workers	174
7-6 Hiring when Unemployment is Low	176
7-7 Hiring Without Resumes	178
7-8 Interviewing Job Applicants	180

7-1 Hiring and Training

Q. What is the best practice for hiring and training new workers?

A. Managers are appraised by higher management, not only for their personal performance, but also on the team performance of the manager and subordinates. A manager can only perform the work that one person can do. If that manager has 10 or 20 subordinates, that manager can multiply their performance by 10 to 20 times by selecting, training, and managing their subordinates well.

Select the very best subordinates available, preferably from existing in-house workers if possible. You know the capability of existing workers best from their past performance. If there's no qualified worker in house, then hire from outside, but realize there's no way to accurately determine the capabilities of job candidates.

Job applicants from inside or outside have soft skills and hard skills. The soft skills are dedication, persistence, learning ability, initiative, flexibility, accountability, energy, and interpersonal skills. Hard skills are ability to perform the job both manually and mentally. Focus on the soft skills because if they have the soft skills, they will learn the hard skills. But if they don't have the soft skills, you can't teach them those.

Pick the best candidate available. There are no perfect candidates. When I was a young military unit commander, my battalion commander insisted I find the perfect candidate for each noncommissioned officer position. I knew already that there are no perfect soldiers, workers or for that matter, managers, or military commanders. All real humans have strengths and weaknesses. It's the manager's job to manage them to emphasize their strengths and minimize their weaknesses. In my experience, most people have moderate strengths and moderate weaknesses. A few of my subordinates had super strengths and super weaknesses. With the right assignment, and the right conditions, they could produce amazingly good work. However, if they had the wrong assignments and the wrong conditions, they produced amazingly bad work. Those you must manage with great focus and caution.

To train your subordinates, observe their performance and coach them on the job in real time. When a task or assignment is complete, critique it by emphasizing what they did well. If there were deficiencies, tell them next time, "I suggest you do it this way instead of that way." Listen to any rebuttal and discuss it to emphasize your point.

7-2 Channels for Hiring

Q. What are the most effective channels for hiring new employees?

A. One survey of job seekers will help answer that question. The channels surveyed were internet job sites, temporary and permanent employment agencies, public channels, referral channels and direct inquiry to employers. Surprisingly, 38 percent of job seekers used only one channel and 26 percent used two channels. Most studies of job seeking effectiveness found it's impossible to tell in advance which channel will produce a job; therefore, it's more effective to use as many channels as possible to improve the chance for success.

The survey asked job seekers which channel they found to be most effective. Thirty-five percent said internet sites were most effective. Those respondents were more highly educated professionals. Nineteen percent said referrals by school alumni, present employees, friends, and relatives was most effective. Blue collar workers tended to rate referrals higher, and professionals rated referrals lower. Twenty percent said direct inquiry with the company was most effective. Seven percent said temporary and permanent employment agencies were most effective.

Of those who rated internet sites as the most effective channel, 70 percent said they used a PC in their search. Thirty-five percent used a smart phone and only 18 percent used a tablet. Those results coincide with results of surveys of online shoppers. Apparently the more serious job seekers and shoppers use a PC. That's probably because the PC screen can display more information.

My career experience in hiring was that effective hiring channels depended on the company's individual situation. You need to analyze and decide which channels work best for your business. What works for others may not be the best for you. For example, temporary and permanent employment agencies were not rated highly in the survey at 7 percent. We often hired temp employees from an agency and later hired them permanently. We also often hired contract employees whose skills and work habits we knew rather than take chances on hiring an unknown new worker. We also relied on referrals by present employees in hiring new employees and found that worked well.

Regardless of what hiring channel you use, it's wise to hire new employees on a probation basis for several months. Train them well and observe their performance and work ethics during the probation prior and if necessary, counsel them on areas of needed improvement. Regardless how rigorous the hiring process, you never know what their performance will be and how well they will fit until you try them.

7-3 Finding Qualified Employees

Q. I'm not finding qualified applicants for my small business. How can I fill my open jobs?

A. On surveys, about a third of small businesses report they can't find qualified workers for their vacant jobs.

Since the recession employers have become very picky about who they hire. Only a third offer to train new workers. The other two thirds think training is too costly. The U.S. labor department has more than 5,000 job titles. It's unlikely an employer will find the perfect candidate that requires no training. Community colleges can't afford to offer training for 5000 job titles. They offer about 100 associate degrees. Businesses need to fill the gap by offering training for jobs specific to their businesses.

Some employers refuse to hire the long-time unemployed thinking they have lost their skills or become unmotivated to work. The long term unemployed are unemployed for reasons beyond their control. Most have exhausted their unemployment insurance and are desperate to work. Other employers reject applicants because they are overqualified for the job. Yes, they might leave when the economy improves but that may be years away. Meantime, the employer gets a bonus from the employee's knowledge and skill that they couldn't afford otherwise.

Other employers avoid hiring older workers. That's a mistake. Baby boomers were born between 1946 and 1964. They make up 30 percent of the workforce. About 10,000 will reach age 65 every day for the next twenty years. That's 3,650,000 each year. They are a very skilled and motivated segment of the workforce. During the financial crisis of 2008 the value of their 401-Ks dropped more than 30 percent and only now are recovering their previous value provided the individual stayed invested. Their home values are still down typically 20 to 50 percent. Many baby boomers have financial motivation to continue working. Because of improvements in medical care and health most baby boomers at age 65 are still in good health.

First, if you have baby boomer employees try to retain them. Only 30 percent of employers are doing that. If you don't have them, try to hire them. You may need to offer reduced work hours, flexible schedules, continued benefits past age 65 and specially tailored job duties. Retirement age baby boomers are excellent trainers, mentors, consultants, and role models for younger employees.

7-4 Hiring New Employees

Q. Online job recruiting is not producing good results for my business. What does work?

A. Choose the right advertising venue for your specific job. Online job board postings trigger an avalanche of e-mail responses from unqualified candidates that must be sorted and screened. Candidates selectively screen online job boards and may respond if a job interests them but are not likely to respond to an ad that requires creating an account to proceed in the application process. Advertise in the local newspaper if the job vacancy is local. It still works. Job seekers read the local ads. Most jobs are filled by referrals from present employees, business friends, suppliers, and customers.

Write an effective ad. Skip the company mission and self-promoting. Candidates will Google your website for that. Include a brief description of the skills, education and experience required. Include a brief job description. I've seen job descriptions in the local paper that were many paragraphs. Use plain English and don't include industry jargon that only insiders understand. Don't overstate your requirements. Some ads seem to be written to exclude as many applicants as possible. Ask for a resume and cover letter first. That tests the applicant's professional writing skills. Don't use online assessments to select candidates for interview. That's too impersonal and demeaning to be screened by a computer program using arbitrary criteria. Most online assessments screen out the good candidates and accept poor ones.

Prepare for each face-to-face interview differently depending on the candidate. You don't interview the new college graduate and the mid-career professional the same way. Ask open ended questions to encourage in depth responses not yes and no responses. The candidate should do 80 percent of the talking. Listen carefully to responses. Determine the candidate's skills, education, and experience. Don't expect perfection. That doesn't exist. If it becomes obvious during the interview that the candidate is not a fit, end the interview with courtesy and explain why. Candidates appreciate the feedback.

Communicate. You represent your business. Acknowledge each candidate's submissions. Notify each candidate you interview with a personal communication the outcome of their application. If not selected, give them helpful feedback to assist their job search. When you find the right person, hire them. Don't drag the process out for weeks and months and keep the applicant dangling. Remember that the intangibles like personality, character, work ethic, interpersonal skills, dependability, and persistence are equally important to job success as tangible things like skills, education and experience. Most jobs can be learned quickly by a candidate with good intangible abilities.

7-5 Hiring Older Workers

Q. Is hiring older workers beneficial for my business?

A. One study predicted that by 2022, 35 percent of the US labor force will be older than 50. That's up from 25 percent in 2002 and 33 percent in 2012. That's because 10,000 baby boomers are reaching age 65 every day and that will continue for many years. The study found that hiring older employees doesn't increase a business's employment cost compared to hiring younger employees. Another benefit is that turnover is lower. The study found that workers age 50 and above had a 29 percent unexpected turnover rate compared to 49 percent for lower age employees.

Older workers have good soft skills. They arrive at work on time, have low absenteeism, communicate well, and are team players. On business surveys, employers rate soft skills as being more important than hard skills. In my career as a plant manager, we generally didn't hire new employees younger than 25 because many had not learned the soft skills.

Many older workers will continue to work for a long time. Because of better medical care, life expectancy is longer and more important older people remain mentally and physically active to a much later age than previously. The financial crises and great recession reduced the value of worker's 401-Ks and many need to work longer.

Older workers have valuable experience and experience counts. Experience counts in several ways. Experienced workers make fewer mistakes. They have learned from past mistakes and don't repeat them. They complete tasks quicker. The first time we do a task takes longer. Repetition reduces the time required a lot. They avoid going down dead ends and wasting time. If the task requires accuracy, they are more accurate. They know short cuts to complete the task. Especially for complex tasks, experience is very beneficial. Having done the task many times before, they don't have to spend a lot of time figuring out how to do it. The experience of older workers is a valuable resource for younger workers. Teaming older workers with younger workers results in a more productive team.

With all of that said, try to hire older workers who are still motivated to learn and improve their skills. Otherwise, 20 years of experience can be one year's experience repeated 20 times doing things the same way.

7-6 Hiring when Unemployment is Low

Q. As the economy improves and unemployment declines, my business finds it harder to hire qualified workers. How can I fix that problem?

A. Train your own workers. That's what businesses have always done when qualified workers were scarce. The US Labor Department has a list of over 5500 job titles. It's unrealistic to expect community colleges and trade schools to be able to train that many job titles. At best, they can train for approximately 200 job titles that are most common and in demand in their market area. One survey indicated two-thirds of small businesses are spending more time training new workers compared to a year ago. One manufacturing business found it takes six months now to train the average new worker compared to 3 months several years ago. The number of manufacturing workers who quit their job is at an 8-year high because jobs are more plentiful now.

There are soft job skills and hard job skills. Soft job skills are attributes like self-discipline, persistence, and loyalty. Hard skills are knowledge of the job and the hard skills required to do the job. Since you are going to train the worker in the hard skills anyway, hire based on good soft skills. A worker with good soft skills will learn the hard skills, but if they lack the soft skills, you can't teach those. They are inherent attributes of the person and not subject to being taught.

There are numerous ways to train new workers. First have good written procedures for important work and safety functions. Use formal classroom training for teaching vocational math and theory. Then use one on one on the job training by assigning the worker to work with an experienced employee. Have a check list for the trainer to follow to insure they don't overlook important topics. Then assign the worker to work on their own, but have the supervisor continue to observe and coach the new worker when they need help. Rotate the new worker assignments to insure they learn to perform all tasks required by the job.

To train new workers in high skill jobs like welding or computer-controlled metal working machines, send the worker to a certification course at a vocational school or community college. Those schools now offer many certifications courses for high skill jobs where the student learns specific skills for that job.

7-7 Hiring Without Resumes

Q. I've heard that some businesses don't use resumes of previous work experience in hiring new employees. Is that a good idea?

A. Some businesses believe resumes create bias in the hiring process and cause them to hire the wrong person for the job or overlook more capable new hires. It's called "blind hiring". Instead, some businesses ask the applicant to perform an assignment such as writing a software program or other task and judge their performance. That might work for professional specialist such as computer programmers, graphic artists, or architects, but most business tasks require too much in house knowledge of the company business that an applicant would not have. Also, a downside is the applicant may feel the business is trying to get free professional work and resent it. Performing a task is also time consuming for the applicant and the interviewer.

Some businesses only hire applicants who graduate from certain elite universities and have worked for large well-known companies. Being that restrictive is probably not productive. Studies have shown that graduates from certain good state public universities are more successful than graduates of elite universities. On the other hand, some large companies are well known for their graduate training and development programs. Their employees are sought by their competitors.

A good resume provides a record of the candidate's previous work experience and progression to more responsible "jobs". It also shows whether the candidate has been a job hopper not staying in any job long enough. In my career I found professionals needed about 2 years in a new responsible job to learn the job. They are at their most creative and innovative stage for the next 3 years and after that settle into a repetitive mode. A good resume will show that. I can't imagine not reviewing an applicant's resume.

I found that regardless how long and thorough the hiring process for professional employees, you really don't know how they will perform until you try them. There is no way to identify poor or good performers in advance. If you think you can design a fool proof hiring process, you're deceiving yourself. Referrals by present employees or by trusted friends in the industry are good sources for new hires. Referrals and good resumes are the best tools in hiring.

7-8 Interviewing Job Applicants

Q. What are good interviewing techniques for job applicants for my business?

A. A good job applicant interview should have 5 stages. First, make the applicant feel welcome and comfortable. Second, conduct fact finding to determine the applicant's education, training, experience, skills, accomplishments, and career goals. Have a carefully prepared list of questions that you use with all applicants. That creates consistency and enables you to compare the interview questions with later job performance and tweak your questions. Only ask legal questions not age and family situation questions. Ask open ended questions not yes or no questions or questions with an obvious answer. Don't ask trick or trapping questions.

Be a good listener. The job candidate should do 80 percent of the talking. Write down the question answers in shorthand form and later evaluate and score the answers. Limit the interviews to a few not 10 or 15. Don't have the candidate interview with employees who will work for them if they are hired. That produces biased results. Practice your interview skills with present employees acting as job applicants. If you hire a lot of employees, you may want to hire an interview coach which will cost several thousand dollars.

Third, identify the candidate's strengths and weaknesses. Nobody's perfect. In my career I had a couple of bosses who only wanted to hire or promote the perfect candidate. That's unrealistic. That person doesn't exist. It's your job as owner or manager to maximize each employee's strengths and minimize their weaknesses by the tasks, responsibilities, and authority you give them. Don't pick only people like you. Instead, if you're picking a key employee pick someone whose strengths compensate for your weaknesses. That makes the team stronger. Don't assume that the applicant is a fit because their resume fits the job description. The resume lists the candidate's cognitive skills - what they know. Job success also depends on non-cognitive skills like persistence, self-control, focus, time management and initiative.

Fourth, identify the keys that will make the candidate successful in the job. The keys to success may be cognitive skills like knowledge, experience, and training as well as non-cognitive skills like teamwork, people skills, initiative or time management. A candidate with superior technical skills but poor people skills may be the best choice for a job where the employee works alone and has little contact with other employees or customers. That candidate would not be a good choice for a job where the employee works with other employees as a close-knit team that requires constant coordination and collaboration among the team.

Fifth, ask the candidate whether they are interviewing other companies and if they would accept an offer if made. Their answer will indicate how serious they are about the job. In sales that's called closing by getting at least a tentative commitment.

CHAPTER EIGHT

OTHER GOOD ADVICE

SUMMARY

- Be a good listener.

- Bragging done right is ok.

- Control your temper. Anger puts you at a disadvantage.

CHAPTER 8
OTHER GOOD ADVICE

8-1 Accepting Credit Cards	184
8-2 Advantages and Disadvantages of Self Employment	186
8-3 Anger in Business	188
8-4 Artificial Intelligence for HR	189
8-5 Avoid Qualifier Statements	191
8-6 Avoiding Temper Blow Ups	193
8-7 Being a Good Listener	195
8-8 Being Candid	197
8-9 Bragging Done Right	199
8-10 Bring About Change in Business	201
8-11 Bureaucracy in Business	203
8-12 Business Association Membership	205
8-13 Business Collaborations	207
8-14 Business Non-compete Agreements	209
8-15 Conference Call Best Practices	211
8-16 Controlling Anger in Business	213
8-17 Controlling Stress	215
8-18 Coping with a Demanding Boss	217
8-19 Coping with Rapid Growth	219
8-20 Critiquing Myself	221
8-21 Cyber Security	223
8-22 Demanding Bosses	225
8-23 Employee Theft	227
8-24 Favoritism in the Workplace	229
8-25 Feeling Overwhelmed	231
8-26 General Manager Promotion	233
8-27 How Can I be More Innovative?	235
8-28 How Can I be More Productive?	237
8-29 How to say no	239
8-30 Imagination and Innovation	241
8-31 Innovation Processes	243
8-32 Learning from Business Competitors	245
8-33 Optimism and Pessimism in Business	247

8-1 Accepting Credit Cards

Q. Should I accept credit cards in my new business?

A. Yes. Customers expect to use their credit cards and they usually spend 16 percent more when using cards. Yet, 55 percent of the 27 million small businesses still don't accept credit cards. If you do, it gives you a competitive advantage.

By making arrangements with the credit card company, you can accept payments by mobile phone, online or in person. Your credit card processer provides you access to the payment network. A good processer makes sure you get paid. Choose a processer that fits your business size and handles internet sales if you sell online. The bank will verify the customer is good for the payment and transfer the money to your business bank account digitally. The transfer is fast, safe and guaranteed.

By accepting electronic payments, you can compete with competitors by maximizing the customer's choices, convenience, and safety. You get paid faster than by check. You don't have the safety risk of handling cash.

Select your processer carefully. The processer will typically supply the software and hardware to accept electronic payments. Determine the services you need, get price quotes, and compare services and fees. Ask your business's bank about the services they provide and any fees.

Card payments give you quick access to your money and prompt accurate account statements and balances. You and your customers are protected from fraud and theft. Your customers get their money back if someone uses their card fraudulently and you are not liable for those transactions.

Credit cards provide 30 days of free credit without interest payments to the card holder. That's a very valuable asset to customers who are on a tight budget. Many credit card holders use them because the credit card company will defend them if they have a dispute with the vendor and decide to cancel the purchase. Stay on good terms with the credit card companies. Your business can't afford to be blacklisted by the credit card company because of a dispute with a customer over a transaction. Credit cards are so important for your business you can't afford to be cut off by the credit card company. Credit cards do cost you about 2 to 3 percent of the sale as a processing fee, however they are worth that to you.

8-2 Advantages and Disadvantages of Self Employment

Q. What are the advantages and disadvantage of being self employed?

A. Self-employed people are referred to as independent contractors. Self-employed make up about 7 percent nationally of businesses.

Highly skilled self-employed like Engineers, Doctors, Attorneys and Accountants have skills that are in demand and typically do well. Low skill workers are often self employed by necessity not by choice and often don't do as well as employees with similar skills who are working for a company. Middle skills like plumbers, electricians and HVAC technicians can also do well if they have a good customer base to keep them busy.

The major disadvantages are as follows; The self-employed have to pay both the employee and the employer portion of social security and Medicare taxes. The employer portion is 7.65 percent of income. That's deductible from your personal income tax return which depending on your tax bracket nets out to about 6 percent.

The self-employed pay the full cost of their personal and family medical insurance. Depending on the plan you choose that can be about $5,000 a year for you and $10,000 additional for your family. Your medical insurance cost for most self-employed is not tax deductible but is deductible to the employer if you are a company employee. Many self-employed work for a single customer or at most several customers. If the customer's business revenue goes down due to company problems or a business recession, the self-employed are usually the first to be terminated.

The major advantages are as follows; The self-employed can deduct legitimate business expenses on their personal tax return. However, most self-employed don't have a lot of deductible business expenses which limits that benefit. Self-employed have several choices of tax deferred savings plans including the Solo 401(K) or the Self-Employed IRA.

Depending on the plan you choose you can save tax deferred $17,500 per year to $52,000 per year. Company employees can't save anywhere near those amounts. That's a major benefit for high income self-employed like Engineers, Doctors, Attorneys and Accountants. It's not a significant benefit for low-income self-employed because they can't afford to save large amounts. You choose your investments like low-cost stock and bond index funds while company employees have limited choices as determined by the company.

The Affordable Care Act (ACA) prohibits medical insurance companies from rejecting applicants based on pre-existing conditions and they cannot charge more for pre-existing conditions. Low-income self-employed qualify for major government subsidizes that reduce annual premiums as low as several hundred dollars depending on income.

Self-employment is especially beneficial for the high income high skilled.

8-3 Anger in Business

Q. Can anger be beneficial in business negotiation?

A. Researchers who study negotiation skills say yes, but you must follow certain rules, otherwise anger can be a fault not a benefit. First, stay in control of your anger. Yelling, name calling, swearing, and accusing don't work. Always express your anger in a calm and controlled way. Second, pick your timing. Hold your anger until the negotiation begins or better still for a decisive point in the negotiation when anger may win a concession from the other party. Getting angry in advance will distract you and drain you emotionally.

Third, define your objective and stay focused on the objective. Focus on what will make the situation better not on winning. The best outcome for a business negotiation is a win-win for both parties. Each party gets it's must have issues. That ensures that the agreement reached will be diligently executed by both parties.

Fourth, believe that anger will work for you. If you have confidence, you will be more confident and assertive and make stronger arguments for your case. If you think it won't work, don't do it.

Fifth, avoid anger if your objective is to find a creative solution to the issue. Anger narrows your focus. Anger doesn't allow us to use our minds in a fast-flowing way to think creatively.

Sixth, in my career I found it useful at times to express anger at a situation, condition, or problem, but never at a person. Others will understand your anger at a situation, condition or problem and may even empathize with your anger, but anger at a person will always be perceived as unfair and unjustified.

I also learned in my business career that it's a waste of time to try to negotiate an agreement with another party when that party has no desire or intention of reaching an agreement.

8-4 Artificial Intelligence for HR

Q. I've read and heard a lot about computer artificial intelligence. Can computers really do HR functions like recruiting, retention and worker evaluations?

A. There's a lot of hype in the press about artificial intelligence (AI). Computers are lightning fast and super for some things. However, scientists still don't understand how the human brain uses electrical signals between billions of brain cells to produce what we call human intelligence. If we don't understand human intelligence, it's unlikely a computer programmer can create an AI program to do what the human does. We need to adopt a wait and see attitude. Use AI for what it can do well but recognize its limits and be skeptical. The human business manager ultimately must decide whether what comes out makes sense.

Computer AI programs can search 100s of applicant resumes and based on pre-programmed criteria and job descriptions select those for the HR manager to consider. However, that depends on the pre-programmer selecting the right criteria. The HR manager better analyze the criteria skeptically or they may miss the best candidate.

There are AI programs that will review a worker's e-mails and based on pre-programmed criteria, identify workers who are disgruntled and likely to leave. Again, if the criteria are wrong, the result is garbage. Also, the worker won't be happy that the business is snooping in their e-mails when they find out. There are privacy issues involved in any AI monitoring of workers or customers.

There's an AI program that will analyze how likely a worker is to leave based on criteria like time since last promotion, time since last raise, time off taken and numerous other criteria.

Another AI program can track how workers use their computer web browsing, e-mails, chat, document, and app use. Based on how all the business's computers are used the AI calculates a base line for the activities and signals when a particular worker is exceeding base line (such as hours spent on Amazon or malicious activity-repeated failed password entries). The AI alerts the business of suspicious activity that may indicate poor productivity and use of time. One multimedia business uses that AI program to monitor worker's work on projects and re-directs the worker when needed. If you use that kind of AI monitoring, tell workers in advance they will be monitored and maybe even ask them to sign an acknowledgement of that.

8-5 Avoid Qualifier Statements

Q. I have a bad habit of using a lot of qualifiers when I talk to other businesspeople, and it tends to offend them. How can I break that habit?

A. There are dozens of qualifiers phrases some people use. It's a habit that adds nothing to communication and often confuses or offends the other person. One type is disclaimers that like legal disclaimers attempt to absolve the speaker for responsibility for what they say. Have you ever heard anyone start out with "Don't take this the wrong way" and heard anything nice? Another disclaimer is "I'm only telling you this because I like you". A sentence starting like that never ends well. The person on the receiving end of that is not going to like the speaker when it's over. Disclaimers never absolve the speaker of responsibility for what follows and can only damage relationships. They really convey a spiteful or vengeful attitude on the speaker's part.

Another type of qualifier confuses the other person. When the speaker starts with "I want you to know" or "I'm just saying" the following sentence is always unclear and confusing. The speaker often really means the opposite of what they say. Those qualifiers often signal bad news, criticism or the speaker's dishonesty. What purpose is there in saying "I just want to say you made a great presentation?" If the speaker is sincere, just say, "you made a great presentation."

Other qualifiers signal that the speaker is about to lie. The phrase "I am writing to say" at first seems harmless. However, it often signals that the following statement is a lie. At the least it's totally unnecessary. The writer's purpose in writing should be evident by what they write and needs no stated purpose up front. The fourth kind of qualifier avoids commitment. Both "I am thinking that" and "As far as I know" mean that the speaker or writer are not committed to what follows. They are often used in writing letters, memos, reports and e-mails to avoid accountability. In my business career I occasionally received memos and reports from others that had so many qualifiers, conditions and exceptions that what they said was meaningless. Legal documents are usually a maze of qualifiers and disclaimers to the point that what's certain is a very small sliver. That's the reason a friend says never, ever ask an attorney to make a business decision.

To break the habit of using qualifiers make a list of all those you use and review it daily. Then train yourself to think before you speak. Consider how the other person will perceive what you say. Remember that qualifiers always impede good communication. If a person is unwilling to stop using qualifiers, that may be an indication that person wants to avoid responsibility and accountability. That's a character problem not a speech problem.

8-6 Avoiding Temper Blow Ups

Q. I have a hot temper. How can I avoid blowups with other employees, customers, and suppliers?

A. Situations that lead to temper blowups almost never develop instantly. They develop over a long time and the two parties finally explode. Don't let friction fester and become more and more intense. Recognize friction early on and try to resolve it with the other party. If a blowup does occur, each party needs to recognize that the other party is acting from feelings of resentment, unfairness, and mistreatment. Neither party acts logically nor rationally. Both parties need to vent their feelings and listen to the other person's complaints. Venting reduces the emotional tension. After both parties have vented and calmed down negotiate a settlement of the dispute.

If the blowup occurs with others present, the parties should immediately retire to a private space where they can't be observed or heard. Having others present inflames both parties because their egos and images are at stake. It's more difficult or impossible to work out differences. Having others present creates a major disruption of the workplace causing loss of productivity and anxiety among the employees who witness the blowup. Observers may later use what was said during the blowup as leverage to gain favors from the two parties. Having witnesses' damages both parties' professional reputation and credibility. Never blowup with clients or customers present. Surveys indicate 80 percent of clients and customers who witness a blowup between two employees will never buy from that business again.

Address your anger at the other person's conduct and behavior that causes your personal problems. Avoid making angry statements about the other person's character, honesty, or integrity. Those are very hard to take back after you reconcile your differences. Ask your common boss to mediate and resolve disputes between the two parties. Experienced managers mediate disputes between subordinates often and become skilled in doing so. It's part of the job of managing. They also have the advantage of being objective authority figures which gives them clout with both parties. If your business has a human resource manager, ask that manager to mediate. Human resource managers are typically skilled mediators.

Try to reach a mutual agreement that both parties can live with. After venting, apologies by both parties are very effective in resolving emotional issues between two parties. Experienced mediators know that after emotional issues are resolved, it's relatively easy to resolve factual issues. Put the agreement in writing. Humans easily forget the terms of verbal agreements and that leads to later follow on disputes.

Mediators find that about 85 percent of voluntary agreements between two parties to resolve disputes are honored by both parties. That compares to about 90 percent of court orders to resolve disputes between two parties are not honored by one or another of the parties. Reaching voluntary agreement makes all the difference.

8-7 Being a Good Listener

Q. How can I be a better listener when communicating with employees, peers, suppliers, and customers?

A. Most of us are poor listeners. Studies indicate we remember only about 10 percent of what we hear in conversation. There are reasons why we are poor listeners. Most of us can think about twice as fast as the other person talks. Our mind wanders. Often, we are thinking about what we want to say next instead of listening. Some only listen if they agree with what's being said. Others interrupt with opinions before they understand what's being said.

We prejudge what's being said based on our assumptions, beliefs, and expectations. We prejudge the other person's information because we think they aren't a creditable source. People in authority tend to dismiss what subordinates say. Mobile smart phones and social media cause interruptions that interfere with listening. People don't remember what they hear because they assume, they can google it later.

Businesspeople can teach themselves to be better listeners. Spend 80 percent of the time listening and 20 percent talking. Before a planned conversation empty your brain by writing down your to do list and key information you want to return to later. Prepare a list of questions and topics. Strive to keep an open mind. Don't assume you already know what will be said. Turn off mobile communication devices to avoid interruptions.

During the conversation take notes to keep you focused on what's being said. Rephrase what you think you hear and ask whether your interpretation is correct. If you don't completely understand, ask questions to clarify your understanding. Pay attention to the other person's body language, tone of voice and facial expressions. They convey a lot of non-verbal information. Allow pauses in the conversation. The other person is likely to feel the need to fill the pause with more useful information.

If the conversation is about important things like customer complaints, planning sessions, project plans or negotiations, write a brief summary of key bullet points after the conversation. Without a written summary the two party's memory of the conversation will be very different and that can lead to future ongoing disputes. You'll be surprised how much written bullet points will jog your memory to recall details.

Nowadays, many businesses are too complex for the manager or owner to have all the information and skills to run the business alone. You need to use all information available from creditable sources like customers, employees, suppliers, your banker, and accountant. To get that information you need to be a good listener. Being a good listener conveys to the other person that you welcome their input and participation and that creates a good relationship between your business and that person.

8-8 Being Candid

Q. I read a business journal article about some businesses that encourage workers to be very candid about the behavior and performance of co-workers and managers. Would that be good for my business?

A. Some businesses do encourage what they call radical candor or "front stabbing". In my business experience, I found it better not to adopt every new business fad. Some fads cause a lot of disruption and damage, fail to work well, and are soon abandoned. Better to wait to see which fads survive the test of time and become regular business practices. That's especially true with employee behavior with each other and with their managers.

The theory is that radical candor between co-workers and between managers and subordinates produces productive change in the employee criticized that benefits the business and the employee working relationships. However, it also has the potential to create enemies and broken relationships. A business adopting such a program should have a good consultant to set the ground rules and train the employees. Otherwise, the employee criticized will likely take the criticism as a personal attack.

Traditionally, managers are expected to criticize the behavior and performance of subordinates when it's necessary for the welfare of the business. That's generally recognized as being fair and necessary. However, when co-workers criticize each other or their manager, the motivation is suspect whether it's for the good of the business or for personal reasons unrelated to business. Traditionally, if a worker thinks a co-worker's behavior or performance is damaging the business, the worker makes that complaint to the manager who determines whether it is valid and if valid counsels the co-worker.

Most workers are very reluctant to criticize the behavior and performance of co-workers or their managers. They fear being branded as disgruntled and uncooperative employees.

It seems most businesses that have adopted such policies are professional practices like engineering, consulting, advertising, accounting, and attorney practices. In such businesses the success of the business depends on the performance of each employee since they work independently with customers and co-workers may be in a better position to see the co-worker behavior and performance than the manager. Still, it would seem that the traditional way of reporting behavior and performance issues to the manager to handle would be better to keep harmony in the work place. In most businesses the worker doesn't work independently with the customer. Instead, they work as teams and it's the team's performance that counts not the individual performance. However, it is important that workers feel free to speak up when they see things that are not good for the business without fear of reprisal.

8-9 Bragging Done Right

Q. Should I brag when I have success in my business?

A. Bragging done right can be good in business, but bragging done wrong can be bad. Research shows that bragging done right will cause others to see you as competent. Staying silent about your achievements causes others to see you as humble but less competent. You can use bragging to manipulate how others see you. Ask yourself, "do I want to be seen as competent or as moral in this situation?"

There are rules for using bragging effectively. Choose your occasion. On this occasion do you want to be seen as competent or as moral and likeable? Never exaggerate – Can you back up your claim or at least are you safe from being proved wrong? Don't take credit for other's success. Don't compare yourself with others – That expresses superiority and a negative attitude toward others. Others will resent that. Tell a story – Make the story interesting and slip in a little bragging. It's less conspicuous that way. Limit using "I" – Sometimes you must start with "I" but used too often and you sound insufferable. Share the credit with others. Be passionate and enthusiastic – Saying I'm proud of this and want to share it is a good start. Practice makes perfect – Rehearse your bragging beforehand and decide exactly what you will say. Don't go on and on, use a monotone or ramble. Move on quickly.

If your boss is in another location and you seldom meet, it's critical to keep your boss informed of your progress and accomplishments. Early in my career, I assumed my boss would observe and recognize my good work and I shouldn't have to lower myself to brag about it. That turned out to be very wrong with an absentee boss and my first career with a company ended in early retirement. I recognized my failure and with my second company, I was very proactive promoting my plant and myself. A manager really owes it to his subordinates and himself to ensure that higher management understands and appreciates the groups accomplishments.

If you follow the rules, it won't be perceived as bragging. It will be perceived as good reporting to keep the boss informed about the operation. Bosses like good reporting because it prevents them from being blindsided by bad surprises. Being blindsided makes your boss appear to upper management as being out of the loop and not in control. During your daily reporting emphasize the successes of yourself and your subordinates and follow the rules. You'll get the message through and not appear to be bragging.

8-10 Bring About Change in Business

Q. I am a very loyal, dedicated employee but sometimes disagree when my company does something that I think harms the business. How can I express my disappointment and try to effect change?

A. A recent survey measured worker attitudes toward their work. Thirty percent reported they were actively engaged meaning loyal, committed, and involved. Fifty percent said they were not actively engaged meaning doing their jobs and no more. Twenty percent were actively disengaged meaning they disliked their work and employer. Among college graduates the similar percentages were 40, 50, 10.

Actively engaged employees are loyal, proud of their company, feel they belong to the company and are disappointed and offended if the company does something they disagree with or violates what they feel are their common values and standards. They are called "organization lovers". At a social occasion, if asked what they do, they will likely name the company they work for. You are obviously one of the engaged.

A lot of business success is about picking the battles you can win and avoiding those you can't win. To pick winners try to control your emotions and analyze the issue logically and calculate your chances of bringing about change. Some companies and managers are more receptive to key employee feedback than others. Good managers vet decisions with subordinates and consider their input especially if the decision will impact the subordinate.

You are not likely to change major company decisions and projects after they are launched. You may be able to influence future decisions and projects by being asked for input during the decision-making process. If you know a decision is being considered, ask for an opportunity to have input. If your boss says no and you've done it in a professional way, there's no harm done.

If you do decide to try to bring about change, don't go it alone. You may be perceived as a complainer or wanting to advance your own agenda. Recruit and persuade co-workers of like mind to support you. Start with your boss even though the decision you object to was made by a manager of another department or higher management.

Your manager will likely resent being bypassed if you don't talk to your manager first. Your manager may know something that affected the decision that you don't know and that will avoid you making a accusation that's unfounded.

The best choice may be to say nothing especially if it's a sensitive area like a promotion, demotion, or discipline. Managers can't discuss those with other employees. If you do know that someone in the company is acting unethically or illegally, take it to your manager or Human Resources.

When contesting a decision recognize that you too could be wrong or be misinformed about the issue. If after giving your input the decision stands, it's your obligation to make a good faith effort to make it work.

8-11 Bureaucracy in Business

Q. How can I eliminate bureaucracy and encourage innovation in my business?

A. Bureaucracy is not always bad. There are situations where bureaucracy is essential to avoid costly or catastrophic mistakes. Manufacturers who make and sell high risk things like car seats and cribs for children must have rigorous bureaucratic systems to ensure that each product designed, manufactured and sold is absolutely safe in every situation where it may be used. Otherwise, the manufacturer is subject to costly and catastrophic class action lawsuits. Industries like oil & gas, oil refining and chemicals handle flammable materials that are subject to leaks and fires. They are also subject to thousands of EPA environmental regulations and OSHA safety regulations. EPA and OSHA demand 100 percent compliance in every case.

Manufactures of complex products like cars and airplanes have vast logistical supply systems that stretch around the world. They must have rigorous bureaucratic systems with centralized control and standard processes and procedures to ensure the right parts with the right specifications and quality arrive just in time at the assembly line. Otherwise, chaos shuts the operation down. Can you imagine the chaos that would result if each fast-food restaurant made its own menu? We even need to cut government bureaucracy a little slack because many of their services like airport security and food inspection must deliver perfect results. Government also must treat each citizen exactly alike to avoid favoritism and that precludes flexibility to be more reasonable based on the situation.

As with many things in business it's a matter of keeping the right balance between bureaucracy and flexible innovation. Small businesses usually have minimum bureaucracy because they are simpler businesses with few employees all in one location and produce products or services that have minimum risks. However, if a small business sells goods and services to a large bureaucratic business, it will have to comply with the customer's bureaucracy.

There are several ways to reduce bureaucracy. If safety or regulatory compliance are not an issue, eliminate the process and see what happens. For example, stop making the report and see if anyone complains. Always try to meet a requirement in the simplest way possible involving the fewest workers. Normally the lowest level worker who has the knowledge and skill required should make the decision and handle the assignment. Use "information only" copies of memos, e-mails, and texts to those who need to know but not participate. Each additional worker you involve in a process greatly increases the time required for communication, collaboration and sign off. Unfortunately, in some businesses and in government it seems they involve the most people possible in each process. If a process requires 100 percent performance every time, assign it to one worker. Dispersing it among many workers fails because each assumes the other did it.

8-12 Business Association Membership

Q. Is membership in chambers of commerce, business associations and trade associations worthwhile for my small business?

A. Yes. A recent article in a business journal about the advantages of franchise businesses joining chambers of commerce illustrates the many benefits. Those benefits also apply to all small businesses and to memberships in local business associations and trade associations. A 2007 study identified the benefits. They conducted a survey of 2,000 randomly chosen consumers who said that knowing a small business belonged to its local chamber of commerce increased by 63% the likelihood the consumer would be a repeat customer. Half of the consumers surveyed said they were more likely to eat at a restaurant if it was a chamber member. However, you shouldn't use your membership to blatantly market your business. Find subtle ways to make customers aware of your membership.

Such business associations offer many opportunities to network and build relationships with other businesses and potential customers. Not only is networking a good marketing tool but it's also a good source for information, advice, encouragement, support and help in identifying best business practices. There are many networking opportunities: after hours mixers, events, committees, workshops, ribbon cuttings, monthly member lunch meetings and fund-raising events. Networking can produce useful information about interest rates, wage rates, inflation rates, GDP growth, changing customer tastes and credit availability that affect all businesses to some degree. Networking can also keep you informed about local business conditions like major construction projects, new competition, customers and suppliers, taxes and regulations that affect your business. Participation in a business association is a long-term process. Don't expect immediate benefits.

Membership in business associations gives your small business representation on local and national business issues that you couldn't attain otherwise. Business associations enable small businesses to pool their resources and hire professional staff to represent their interests by lobbying government officials at the local, state, and federal level to ensure that their members are not unfairly penalized by government laws and regulations. Be an active member of your local business associations which concentrate on local business issues and problems. Recognize that the local business association represents the interests of all its members not just your business. They cannot support your issues if they conflict with the interests of the other members. There are active business associations in most areas of Cities that do a good job for their members.

Many business associations offer other benefits. Some offer health insurance at lower rates than individual businesses could obtain. You benefit from being in the association's large risk pool that spreads the risk over tens of thousands of employees. Many local associations have monthly newsletters that go to a large, targeted audience of association members and community leaders. Advertising rates in those newsletters are very low considering the size and quality of the circulation. Some association websites receive very large numbers of hits and are good places to advertise.

8-13 Business Collaborations

Q. How important is collaboration in my business?

A. Selective disciplined collaboration can be productive. Unfortunately, some businesses have taken it to the extreme. Their offices are vast open spaces full of cubicles. There are so many distractions nobody can think clearly about serious complex tasks. It's ironic that knowledge businesses that require deep analytical thinking are the most fanatic about collaboration.

Researchers have found even short interruptions increase the time to complete a complex task. One researcher says multitasking reduces efficiency because of attention residue meaning the mind continues thinking about the old task after starting a new one. One researcher found that knowledge workers spend 70-80 percent of their time in meetings, with e-mail and their smartphones. Some collaborators are so busy collaborating on so many projects, they cause a bottleneck and project delays while others wait to hear from them.

One study estimated that each e-mail response costs 95 cents of labor and can add up to $1Million per year for a medium size business. Some managers feel they must be seen to be an effective manager. As a result, they fill up everybody's days with meetings, e-mails and voice mails.

It's telling that the decline in US worker productivity over the past 10-15 years coincides with the popularity of e-mails and smartphones. Various studies have shown some workers spend from 50 to 80 percent of their day on e-mails and smartphones. No doubt most of that time is nonproductive and unnecessary. That's a huge potential saving in time and labor cost.

Individual workers can control their time collaborating by meetings, e-mails, and smartphones by skipping meetings and ignoring e-mails and voicemails that don't require their participation. They can shut down their devices during periods of the workday to provide quite time to work on complex projects. However, some businesses emphasize collaboration so much that workers who do that may jeopardize their chances for promotion. In that case top managers must set policies for employees concerning meeting invitees, e-mail copies and e-mail strings. Policies are not effective if managers at all levels don't follow up and correct workers who violate the policy.

8-14 Business Non-compete Agreements

Q. I lose many of my best sales staff hiring prospects because I require them to sign a non-compete agreement. How can I avoid that?

A. You are probably losing your best sales staff prospects unnecessarily because of your non-compete agreement. Texas court case history is that it's very difficult for an employer to enforce an employee non-compete agreement that prevents the former employee from plying their trade to earn a living. Other States may be similar. At most you may be able to keep the former employee from using your customer list, hiring your employees or using your confidential business information. Not selling to your customers may be questionable if the former employee needs to sell to them to ply their trade and make a living.

There are several downsides to non-compete agreements. It basically requires the new employee to sign over all their new knowledge, experience, and connections they gain while working for you. That knowledge, experience and connections constitute the employee's human professional capital and damages their ability to ply their trade and make a living if they leave you. The non-compete agreement may make the employees feel trapped, dependent, and resentful which causes de-motivation and poor performance. The new employee who's willing to sign away their human professional capital, freedom, and future ability to make a living is probably not the motivated, loyal, productive employee you want. On the other hand, you lose the best prospects because they are in demand by your competitors and won't sign as you are experiencing.

In any event an employee who wants to leave can negate the non-compete agreement by taking a job outside your market area or out of state. In many occupations like sales the customer is loyal to the salesperson not to the business. The customer has a long relationship with the salesperson and has confidence and trust in that salesperson. If the salesperson leaves, the customer is likely to leave regardless of whether the salesperson takes the customer with them or not.

There's also a basic fairness issue. Employers now days have great expectations of new employees. They expect them to have the knowledge, skills, and experience on the first day of employment to be fully productive without any training. However, many employers have zero expectation of employing them long term. Those employers by necessity or to cut costs lay off promptly when the market or business cycle turns down. Not only is the laid off employee out of a job but saddled with a non-compete agreement that impedes their ability to find another job. Non-compete agreements probably should only be used when an employer's principal assets are intellectual property. That can be handled with a non-disclosure agreement rather than a non-compete agreement.

8-15 Conference Call Best Practices

Q. My business has employees and colleagues in several countries around the world. How can I make conference calls more productive?

A. A recent business journal article gave best practices for conference calls. Conference calls are here to stay. Time spent in conference calls is increasing about 10 percent each year and about 65 percent are by phone. It's a very useful tool to cope with growing business globalization and travel costs.

However, complaints about poor conference call etiquette are rampant. Remote participants fail to mute their phones and all sorts of background noise comes through. Remote participants multitask and don't participate. Remote participants fail to build rapport with those on site. One study of 3301 businesspeople indicated 75 percent said building rapport was a serious obstacle. Another 71 percent said lack of participation by remote participants was a problem.

The lack of visual body language and facial expressions makes remote participants reluctant to speak and harder to concentrate. Conflicts are more likely because remote participants feel left out or ignored. Conference call leaders are not mindful that remote participants around the world must get up in the middle of the night to participate.

Good conference call etiquette and best practices help a lot. Conference call leaders should set firm ground rules and tight agendas to keep participants on track. Leaders need prepared written questions to get remote participants talking and write down the answers for later reference. Leaders listen more and talk less than in face-to-face conferences. A good guide is for the leader to talk 40 percent of the time and listen 60 percent.

If remote participants don't know the others, the leader should begin by asking each participant to introduce themselves and say what their role is and what they expect to get out of the conference call. If a remote participant is not talking, the leader should ask them a question to get them talking. Otherwise, they may feel left out and become hostile.

Leaders should ask each participant to state their name before speaking so remote participants know who is talking. Conference calls requiring interaction shouldn't include more than 7 to 9 participants. If larger, participants don't get to talk and feel ignored. Larger groups also encourage multiple conversations within the group.

The leader should be the moderator or appoint another participant to be moderator to keep people on topic and on time. If the remote participants are around the world, the leader should schedule calls to be as convenient as possible for the remote participants and vary the schedule to spread the inconvenience equally.

Video conferencing equipment is becoming better in quality and less expensive. However, video tends to make people self-conscious and they avoid using the video and use voice instead. Some people feel they need to dress up if they are on video.

8-16 Controlling Anger in Business

Q. I sometimes lose my temper with subordinates and suppliers in my business. Is that bad and if so, how can I change?

A. The times for tough, angry, yelling bosses is over. It doesn't work now days and, in my career, I never found it worked. It never makes sense to antagonize people who can hurt you. It's OK to express public anger at a situation but never at an employee or supplier. Others will understand and accept anger at a situation but never at them. Anger at the situation may express what the other person feels, and it can be productive by emphasizing the importance of resolving the situation.

After being angrily reprimanded in public employees are likely to become one of the disengaged who hurt the business more than helping it. They may resign and bad mouth the business in the community and industry. They can use social media to retaliate with bad mouthing comments to hundreds or thousands of people within hours. Your outburst may be caught on smartphone video and spread through the business and outside thus damaging the business's reputation. The next time you need help from the supplier to expedite a delivery or accept late payment that person may retaliate and reject your request for help.

On surveys about 40 percent of employees say they like bosses who are demanding and challenging but also fair and considerate. Surveys also show about 14 percent of US workers report being victims of verbal aggression at work and researchers estimate that may cause $24.8 billion annually in lost productivity, grievance claims, health care cost and lost work time.

Controlling anger in the workplace depends on how well you cope with conflict both on the job and outside your work life. Researchers say workplace anger starts with the annoyances that pile up every day at work and outside. Those are things such as being cut off by another driver in traffic or being on hold waiting for service by phone for 30 minutes or more. Those things trigger anger that you suppress and absorb without an outburst. The anger accumulates until you can't suppress it any longer and respond with an outburst.

There are activities that can replenish your coping capacity. A good night's sleep, recreational activity, exercise, and any enjoyable stress relieving activity will do that. The key to relieving conflict stress at work is not to let it build up to the point of outburst. The outburst at work rarely occurs instantaneously. It's usually the end of a long period of repressed irritations and anger that finally spills over. Talk it out with the other person early and find out why they act that way. It may be something they can't help doing and understanding that may make you more accepting. If you can't work it out, agree to avoid each other as much as possible.

8-17 Controlling Stress

Q. Can I learn to control my stress in my business?

A. Yes. Human behavior research has developed rules for reducing and controlling stress. Research confirms what many of us learn in our career experience. There's healthy, useful stress and there's unhealthy stress. Encourage healthy stress and avoid unhealthy stress. The healthy stress response makes the heart pump faster and releases hormones into the blood stream that boost energy and dampens the digestive and immune systems. Our mind focuses on the threat, and we have the energy to work hard for the duration of the threat. The challenges that create stress are usually new events and situations we've not encountered before. That produces new experiences and skills. The lack of stress creates complacency and repetitive, rote performance. Unhealthy stress is sustained stress that doesn't go away when the threat is over. Sustained stress keeps the heart rate up and blood pressure high which eventually damages the cardiovascular system and impairs the digestive and immune systems.

Your positive attitude toward stress helps. Consider the stressful situations as a challenge and an opportunity to learn and show what you can do rather than a threat. Having control over your work helps a lot. Business owners, managers and professionals who have a lot of control over their work have a lot less stress than production line workers who don't. Finding meaning and purpose in your work helps. Workers in care giving industries like medical and teaching report less stress. Having support and encouragement from your boss and co-workers helps.

Try to avoid situations that trigger stress. Once the stress response fires up it's hard to control and reverse. I spent my career in an industry where a lot of bad things could potentially happen. We spent a lot of time and effort avoiding those. It takes a lot less work to avoid crises than to deal with them after they happen. When they did occur, I had contingency plans to fix the problem or mitigate the consequences. Being prepared boosted my confidence and reduced my stress level. Having hope and optimism helps. Keep the crises in perspective. We tend to exaggerate the bad consequences of a crisis. Look at it not from the perspective of right now or today but over the next weeks or months. What seems important now may not be over the long haul.

Recognize what you can control and what you can't. Many of the things that determine a business's success like market demand, competitive prices, market growth rate, the economic cycle, interests, and inflation rates are beyond your control. Don't beat up on yourself for what you can't control. Be as forgiving of yourself as you would be for a friend or family member.

8-18 Coping with a Demanding Boss

Q. How can I cope with my demanding boss?

A. It can be hard to work for a demanding boss. However, there are potential benefits. Demanding bosses tend to be assigned important company projects because management knows they will produce. By working on important projects, your good work is more likely to be recognized and appreciated by higher management and that helps your career advancement.

First there are "don'ts "in responding to a demanding boss. Don't agree to a demand you know you can't meet. That makes the situation worse because it encourages the boss to continue making unreasonable demands. Instead, try to negotiate a more reasonable deadline or result. Show that you understand the urgency of the request; otherwise, the boss may feel you are to laid back about it and bear down harder. Ask your boss to review the priority of your assignments and tell you which you can delay to have time to focus on the new project. Suggest ways to modify the new project: for example, finishing a part of the project first and the remainder later. Ask the boss whether part of the project could be assigned to a co-worker to reduce your load.

If the boss wants boundless access to your off-duty time, try to negotiate some boundaries. For example, agree to respond to emails, texts, and calls by 9 pm each night rather than interrupt your personal life to respond to each when received. Explain why you need boundaries to protect your personal life and family life. Offer an alternative that is better for you. For example, if the boss wants you to work every Saturday, offer to work 10- or 12-hour days during the week to keep your weekend free.

If the deadline is unrealistic, explain that you are concerned that you can't produce a quality project that quickly.

If your boss persists in making unreasonable demands and refuses to negotiate with you, you may have to decide whether the potential career advancement benefits gained by working for that boss is worth the loss of your personal life. However, try hard to negotiate a better situation first. Type A overachiever bosses tend to not recognize how their demands are affecting the subordinate's personal life. They tend to dedicate their entire life to the job and don't understand that others don't think that way. Careful pushback will often break through their mind set and make them realize they need to back off.

8-19 Coping with Rapid Growth

Q. My business is growing rapidly with revenue growing at 15 percent per year. How do I cope with that growth?

A. At a 15 percent revenue growth rate, your business will double every 5 years. After 20 years, it will be 16 times larger. As the business grows you need to stop being the founder-entrepreneur one person business and become the CEO. That's often hard for founders to do. They just can't let go.

Typically, larger businesses have functional departments: production, marketing, distribution, finance, and accounting, purchasing, and Human Resources (HR). If the business is complex or highly regulated, it will have additional departments. Each function is a specialized technical field and needs a manager with those skills. In a large, rapidly growing business, the founder can't have all the skills needed.

You need to start organizing the business into functional departments and hire a qualified manager for each. Initially, you might want to keep personal control of marketing and finance-accounting because they are the key functions for a successful business. Eventually you will have to turn those over to a manager when the business reaches a certain size.

Give each manager authority and autonomy to decide how to run their functional department. That's delegation and you must learn to delegate. Set up a management control reporting system for each department. Set goals for each year for each department and establish monitoring and measuring reports for you to keep track of progress toward those goals. If a department falls below goals, work with the manager to identify the problems and solutions and take corrective action. Otherwise, monitor departments progress, but don't intervene as long as it's on track.

At some point in the businesses' growth, you will need a board of directors even if you are not a public owned company. Select outside board members who have knowledge and skills that the business needs. Give the board real policy making authority. The board can provide the checks and balances to prevent you from making rash decisions that harm the business. Research has shown that decisions made by a group of well qualified individuals are better than those made by one person. Each of the group has a different perspective on the decision based on their knowledge and experiences.

At some point in growth, you should consider hiring a professional, experienced CEO and you become the Chairman. The CEO can handle the daily business and you can focus on long range planning and strategy.

8-20 Critiquing Myself

Q. How can I critique myself after a task is finished?

A. Psychologist who coach business people recommend talking to yourself. They call it "self-talk". You can do it aloud or silently. In my career, I did self-talk silently. It makes a difference how you do it. You make yourself the target of your own comments, advice, and reminders. Self-talk can be automatic or deliberate. The purpose is to stimulate your action, direct it and evaluate it. Stimulating action is done by motivational self-talk saying, I can do this. Directing action is instructional self-talk. Instructional self-talk is helpful when learning a new task or procedure. For example, if you are giving a talk or presentation, you remind yourself to speak slower and maintain eye contact.

In my career, if I was preparing for a difficult talk like an employee appraisal or presenting a major project for approval, I mentally composed it and rehearsed it almost word for word. I tried to anticipate all questions and prepared an answer. I tried to anticipate the other person's reactions and be prepared to respond. It's easier to respond when you have thought about it in advance.

In evaluating your actions afterword, psychologists say it's helpful to address yourself by name or as "you" rather than "I". Studies find that in performing stressful tasks people perform better if they address themselves as "you" rather than "I". After the task, those who addressed themselves as "you" felt less shame or doubt about their performance.

When evaluating your performance, addressing yourself as "you" makes it easier to give yourself objective, helpful feedback. Avoid being too hard on yourself or using negative terms like "that was dumb". Instead of calling yourself dumb, try to figure out what you did wrong and resolve to not repeat it.

In my career, I found self-talk a good way to prompt my imagination. As a child, I grew up on a farm isolated from playmates. To overcome my boredom, I used my imagination to invent all sorts of adventures. Later in business, self-talk helped me imagine new ways to improve my business. I could work out details of new projects in my mind before I put it down on paper.

8-21 Cyber Security

Q. Is cyber security a big threat to small businesses and how can I defend my business?

A. Yes, small businesses are targets for cyber theft. Typically, about half of small businesses surveyed report being victims in the last year. That's up 44 percent in one year. Cyber criminals target small businesses because they usually have less secure digital systems. A common serious threat is theft of a small retailer's customer credit card numbers. That's typically done by sending malicious emails to business employees inducing employees to download malware that compromises the point-of-sale system. The business is responsible for such customer loss which last year averaged about $21,000 per theft.

Another common theft is sending bogus emails pretending to be from the business owner or CEO authorizing an employee to make a payment to a designated bogus supplier, usually by wire transfer because it's hard to trace the party receiving the payment. The bogus email address is identical to the authentic email address except for an inconspicuous difference like an "i" instead of an authentic "L". Employees should confirm large payments with a phone call or face to face contact with the owner or CEO.

There are many other security measures. Don't click on unknown links, attachments, photos, music or video in emails, smart phones, texts, or websites. Keep computer operating systems and browsers up to date. Use antivirus software and firewalls and update them automatically. Forbid employee personal use of business PCs. Use dedicated PCs for banking activity and don't allow internet surfing or email activity. Never allow the same employee to reconcile accounts and make payments. Reconcile accounts daily and immediately report unauthorized activity to your bank. Regularly back up computer files to avoid lockout or wipe out by malware. Enable popup blockers because criminals use them to install malware. Keep current with news and alerts about cybercrime and risks. Consider cyber liability insurance. Alert employees about cybercrime techniques and red flags to look for.

Banks are concerned about their business customer's cyber security. Ask you bank to help audit your system and procedures.

8-22 Demanding Bosses

Q. Should I be more demanding with my employees, suppliers, and professional advisors?

A. It depends on what you mean by demanding. I never found that yelling, anger, and berating people worked in business or in life. It's OK to be angry at a situation but never at a person. People will understand and relate to your anger at a situation. A business leader or any leader must always have self-control and self-discipline. Yelling, anger, and berating are examples of a person out of control. That behavior never gets a positive response from the other person because it belittles that person. Instead, the other person will respond with anger and resentment. They may not feel they can afford to show their anger and resentment, but they have many ways to retaliate anonymously, and the other party will never know who did it. A well-known example is the airline passenger who berates the ticket agent about a missed connection and the ticket agent routes the passenger's bag to Timbuktu. Your goal is to have a positive response from the other person by teaching and coaching to motivate that person to their best performance.

That doesn't mean that you shouldn't have high standards and expectations of your employees, suppliers, and professional advisors. Your customers expect 100 percent performance each time. Governments expect 100 percent performance from you for safety, environmental and legal compliance. Unfortunately, in school we learn to expect an A for 90 percent performance. In business 90 percent performance will get you fired or if you own your own business 90 percent performance can result in bankruptcy.

High standards and attention to details are essential to attain 100 percent performance. Fortunately, before I became a business manager, I learned that as a company commander in the army reserve from my battalion commander. He demanded 100 percent performance each time from me and my company. No detail seemed to escape his attention. I thought he was unfair and unrealistic. Later as a petroleum refinery plant manager that experience helped me meet the 100 percent expectations from my corporate management and from governmental agencies for safety, environmental and legal compliance.

On the other hand, you shouldn't have unfair expectations of your employees, suppliers, and professional advisors. That has a devastating effect on loyalty, morale, and productivity. They probably won't confront you. Instead, they will go into slow motion. That's passive resistance. Unions call that a slowdown. What used to get done quickly seems to take forever. If you stumble into that situation, reverse course immediately and admit your mistake and apologize.

8-23 Employee Theft

Q. How should I handle cases of employee theft in my small business?

A. Employee theft occurs occasionally in both large and small businesses. It can be a major crisis for a small business because small businesses don't usually have the financial resources to survive an employee theft. I have an acquaintance who lost his business because of employee theft. Theft also damages the mutual trust that small businesses depend on. Handle employee theft carefully to be sure what you do is legal and minimizes the impact on the business.

Experts say it's best to cut ties with the employee quickly. Owners of small businesses tend to want to try to recover the lost assets and give the employees a chance to explain and repay the loss. Experts advise writing off the loss, terminating the employee quickly and explaining the termination as a "downsizing" without mentioning theft.

Accusing the employee of theft requires hard evidence that will stand up in court if the employee sues. Experts say if you don't intend to prosecute, don't accuse the employee of theft. Call it a necessary downsizing. The owner may want to consider offering severance in exchange for a release of claims and a confidentially agreement if the employee has valuable business information.

Make sure there are no other employees involved. If so, terminate all at the same time. That may be a hardship for a small business, but it's necessary to be consistent. Don't discuss the cause of termination with other employees; however, do remind them of the consequences of stealing. Don't tolerate even small theft. That could create a work culture where theft is acceptable. Having good theft monitoring systems is a deterrent.

If the employee is too valuable to the business to terminate, experts advise getting a signed confession and requiring re-payment as a deterrent to prevent future theft. Consider time off without pay as a penalty and put the employee on probation for a period.

Small businesses should review their anti-theft procedures periodically. Whenever possible, have processes that require two or more employees to commit theft. For example, authorize one employee to make purchases, another to receive purchases and third to issue payment. Be especially careful in accounting for each receipt. Cash is easily stolen. Inventory valuable property regularly. Review your bank and credit card statements personally each month. Consider having them mailed to your home if you receive hard copies.

8-24 Favoritism in the Workplace

Q. I have several favorite subordinates that I reward with choice assignments and perks. Is that bad for employee morale and productivity?

A. We usually think of manager favoritism in the workplace as bad for morale, teamwork and productivity. On surveys 75 percent of managers admit favoritism and say that 92 percent of promotions involve favoritism. However, favoritism if used right and for the right reasons can motivate and empower employees in ways that benefit the work team. Research indicates favoritism done right can have the following beneficial affects; better employee self-esteem-employees follow workplace norms of conduct better-employees are more likely to perform tasks that benefit the team-employees are more social-productivity improves. Favoritism works especially well for those employees who will work hard for outward, explicit approval and whose performance lags when not recognized. Human satisfaction is a pyramid. Essential basic needs for shelter, food, clothing, and safety are the base. The top of the pyramid is intangible needs like the need for recognition. Once the lower needs are met the intangible needs are the more powerful motivators for performance. Favoritism done correctly for the right reasons can tap into that need for recognition.

The following rules apply for doing favoritism right for the right reasons. First, the right reasons for favoritism should be to improve the team's job performance, work behavior and productivity. Wrong reasons are to reward those you hired personally over those hired by your predecessor-personal friends outside work-best dressed-owners of pets-all other similar reasons unrelated to the workplace. The wrong criteria convey the message that favoritism is not earned by performance but bestowed based on arbitrary preferences.

Second, tell subordinates what the criteria are. For example, one manager's criteria might be work results, collaboration, kindness, and perseverance. Another manager's criteria might be different depending on the work situation but always related to job performance, work behavior and productivity. Each manager's criteria will likely change from time to time as the situation and manager's goals change.

Third, rotate favorites as they excel in those criteria. It's surprising how much employee performance will change month to month. At one plant I managed we selected an employee of the month based on performance. We rarely had an employee repeat as employee of the month twice in one year. Each employee's challenges and opportunities change month to month and that limits their performance potential. Fourth, when recognizing results don't disparage the work of other subordinates. Also don't compare subordinate's performance publicly. Any discussion of performance should be done privately.

8-25 Feeling Overwhelmed

Q. I feel overwhelmed running my business. How can I fix that?

A. On one survey, 70 percent of business owners felt overwhelmed. They are pulled in too many directions and juggling too many tasks. The key is identifying what's important and working on that first. First- each day pick one important task and get it done in the first hour of the day. Pick the one thing that would have the greatest bottom-line benefit to your business. If it can't be done in one-hour, sub-divide it into one-hour pieces. Second- start your day working on that single task before checking your emails or your voice mails and get it done.

Third- set aside one day each week as a focus day to work on your most valuable project. Important projects take blocks of half days or full days of focused, uninterrupted attention. That means no emails or voice mails or phone calls. Close your door and, if necessary, leave the business site and work some other place. Important complex projects can't be done with constant interruptions. It takes too much time after each interruption to pick up your train of thought.

Fourth- after doing the above, use the time you gained by taking a break. Do something you enjoy. Take a run or go to the park. That gives you time to get things into better perspective.

Fifth-create a stop doing list. We all must do lists. Review your to do list regularly and decide what needs to be deleted or delayed. If an item has been on your to do list for a long time, that probably means it doesn't need to be done.

Sixth- get focused on what matters. In business it's not a matter of doing more. It's about doing better. When you spread yourself too thin on to many things, you don't do anything well. You have a limited amount of time, energy, and attention. You can't afford to waste it on low priority tasks.

Seventh- make a quarterly action plan on one single page of paper.

Pick the top 2 or 3 projects that are most valuable to the business. Identify 3 or 4 measurements of success for each project. Identify 5 to 7 key action steps or milestones for each project. Assign each action step to a subordinate or yourself and show a completion time.

Finally, don't forget to delegate. Tasks should be delegated to the lowest level employee who has the knowledge, experience and authority to complete the task. When delegating, don't forget to follow up. Don't ever assign a task if you are not going to follow up. It's not likely to get done. Follow up doesn't take a lot of time. Doing the task does.

8-26 General Manager Promotion

Q. I have been promoted to general manager of my business. How is a general manager's job different from a department manager's job?

A. Department managers are technical specialist in their area. General managers are generalists who coordinate the activities of all departments to accomplish the business's missions and goals. The failure rate in making that transition is high. The typical departments for a manufacturing business are production, marketing, distribution, purchasing, human resources and finance and accounting. Depending on the nature of your business, there could be more departments like environmental, health and safety and quality control.

As general manager, you don't need to be expert in all those functions. That's the department manager's job. You do need to know generally what each department does. Read the department policy and procedures manual. Discuss and question the activities of each department with the manager. Identify the projects underway in each department. Those projects should have written project action plans that spell out the who, what, why, how, and when and have a project schedule. Read the project action plans and review progress reports to see if the project is on time and on budget. If it's not, discuss the project with the department manager and identify problems and solutions and take corrective action to get the project on schedule and on budget.

The previous general manager should have set up management control reports for each department that monitor and measure the departments' activities. Ideally, those reports should state the goal and the actual performance compared to the goal. If the department is below goal, discuss that with the department manager, identify problems and solutions and take corrective action to get back on track.

If there are no goals or goals are inadequate, establish realistic goals. Give department managers autonomy to decide how to attain their goals. Don't interfere unless progress is unsatisfactory, then identify problems and solutions and take corrective action. Your job as general manager is to monitor progress and intervene only when progress is unsatisfactory or when there are disputes between departments.

Don't try to micromanage your old department by going around or overruling the new department manager. That's unfair to the new manager and bad for business. There's a strong temptation to do that because you know that department's functions so well.

Don't be hesitant to make decisions affecting all the departments because you're not expert in those. Get feedback from each department and proceed with the best option.

8-27 How Can I be More Innovative?

Q. How can I be more innovative in my business?

A. Being able to see analogies between two very different things is a key step in the innovation process. For example, Henry Ford didn't invent the car assembly line process. A Ford employee visited a meat packing plant where the carcasses were moved along a production line where butchers removed different cuts of meat. The employee recognized that process could be used in reverse order to assemble cars. Many of the important breakthroughs in history have come by recognizing that a process that works well for one purpose can also work for a very different purpose. Analogies require comparing two different things and recognizing parallels and connections.

There are several rules for innovating through analogies. Analyze your initial analogy in depth. What seems similar at first may not be. For example, early airplane inventors tried to copy what birds do by flapping wings. The key to flight is not that. It requires forward propulsion to create lift under the wings and a way to control the airplane in flight.

Explore multiple analogies. Don't be satisfied with your first analogy. Look for others that may be better solutions to the problem. Initially Darwin conceived his evolution theory for plants and animals based on a river's ability over eons of time to carve a canyon or valley. The better analogy was selective breeding of domestic animals and plants where the desirable trait was enhanced by future generations.

To develop analogies, consider diverse sources. At first you probably would not recognize the similarity of disassembling animal carcasses and assembling a car. They are totally different industries. But it works.

Simplify. Simple is always better than complex. Unfortunately, many businesspeople try to make things more complex. In my career, I always tried to make things as simple as possible. The desk top computer made computers so simple that anyone can operate them.

Previously computers were monsters in size and operated by highly skilled professionals.

The best innovation is usually small incremental improvements in existing products, services, and processes. It's extremely difficult to invent brand new products, services, or processes. They are rare. It's much easier to make incremental improvements to existing products, services, and processes. The pay back from incremental innovations can be large because it gives you a competitive advantage. However, competitors will duplicate your improvements as soon as possible so it needs to be an ongoing process to stay ahead.

8-28 How Can I be More Productive?

Q. How can I be more productive?

A. Focus on the right things. I credit focus for most of my success in life and business. Psychologists find that when we have a problem or crisis our brains' instinct is to focus on whatever is directly in front of our eyes and grabs our attention. That's called cognitive tunneling. We latch on to the easiest and most obvious stimulus and lose the ability to direct our focus elsewhere.

The following examples illustrate cognitive tunneling with accounts of two aircraft accidents. Several years ago, a plane crashed into the ocean off Brazil. The plane was about to stall, but with all the audible and visual alarms and onboard computer text messages the pilot never recognized the stall. He held the plane's nose up trying to gain altitude until the plane flew into the ocean. It's probably the only plane that ever crashed while under complete pilot control. The other example was a plane that lost 2 of 4 engines on takeoff. It, too, had audible and visual alarms and on-board computer texts. However, the pilot ordered the co-pilot to tell him what systems were working, not what systems were not working. When he got the answer, he realized he could fly and control the plane and land it like he learned to fly a single engine Cessna at the start of his career. He ignored all the distractions, focused on flying, returned to the field, and landed safely. Psychologists believe that people who are skilled at focusing on the right thing have a mental model (plan) of what the situation should look like.

To be productive you must learn to control your focus. In today's business world with all the distractions and interruptions from email, smart phones, texts, and social media, it's surprising any productive work gets done. When you have an important task to do, shut all that down and focus totally on the task. When you have a business problem to solve, first be sure you understand what the real problem is. It's often not what it seems to be because our brain looks for the obvious visible problem. If you focus on the wrong problem, you waste your time and effort and fail just as the Air France pilot failed.

I occasionally get a client who identifies their problem as a shortage of cash, "If only I had more credit all would be well." When I dig into the problem, I usually find the real problem is that the marketing plan is not working to produce enough revenue or the expenses are too high. The client sometimes has difficulty seeing that.

8-29 How to say "No"

Q. I'm very busy both at work and in my personal life. How can I say "no" to requests to take on new jobs without offending the other person?

A. Time is the most valuable thing we have. We need to spend that time in things that are satisfying and rewarding. That doesn't mean pleasurable things. We shouldn't feel guilty about saying no if it's not going to be satisfying and rewarding. After all it's our life and time spent doing something we're not obligated to do is time not spent in things that really count in life. We need to say no to protect our business and personal agendas and priorities to accomplish what we need to accomplish.

That said, many of us feel guilty when we say no. It's caused by our fundamental need for social connection and feeling part of a group. We feel that saying no may threaten that relationship by offending the other person. It may, if not done well. To the other person it means rejection. Rejection is negative and Neuroscience has shown our brains react more to the negative than to the positive.

Negative memories are stronger and long lasting to help us avoid similar experiences in the future. Psychologists say we tend to believe others will judge us more harshly than they do. We think the consequences are worse than they are. Because of guilt, saying no one time can make that person more likely to say yes, the next time.

There's a gentler way to say no. If you know a request is coming, rehearse saying no ahead of time. If you are prepared, you're less likely to cave in. Being prepared you're more likely to use words that won't offend the other person.

If the request is a surprise, buy time by saying I'll think about it and get back to you. That shows you're not arbitrarily saying no but only after careful consideration. It also prepares the other person for a rejection and gives you time to put aside guilt feelings and think rationally before deciding.

Use a gentle tone of voice when saying no. Explain why you can't say yes with things like your workload, project deadlines or other prior business or personal commitments. For example, as a retiree I say no to requests for additional volunteer work by saying I'm as busy as I want to be doing things I enjoy and would have to give up something to take on the new job.

That softens the rejection for the other person and helps your guilt feelings. If the other person refuses to take no for an answer, repeat as many times as necessary. Eventually, the person will get tired and bored and give up. Don't say no but maybe next year or next time unless you really mean it. That only guarantees a future follow up.

8-30 Imagination and Innovation

Q. How important is imagination in successful innovation?

A. Imagination is a personal trait. Innovation is a process that can be taught and learned. The innovation process consists of association, questioning, collaboration, observing and experimenting. Imagination is a key part of the association step which means applying the solution to one problem to solve an unrelated problem that's not similar.

Imagination is a modern development dating from about the early 1800s. Up until then the world consisted of the upper one percent ruling class and the other 99 percent of everybody else. The 99 percent were not allowed to imagine a better future or better way of doing things. That changed with the advent of democracy. A lot of businesses still don't value, encourage, and reward imagination from their employees. It's regarded more as an unproductive waste of time.

Human behavior researchers think about a third of our imagination and creativity are inherited in our DNA and the other two thirds is learned from our life experiences. That indicates that greater variety in our work, social, cultural and education lives helps our imagination. Throughout history people living in trade center cities with diverse cultures and contact with people from other regions have tended to be more imaginative and creative. A broad education no doubt helps. Reading non-fiction in diverse fields like history, economics, science, politics, and travel helps.

A good imagination requires good information sources. An example of good information leading to imagination and innovation is the 1665 London Plaque. The King started requiring a death certificate for each deceased stating cause of death. Doctors started seeing patterns in the data and that led to identifying causes of diseases and treatments. Three industries - statistics, life insurance and public health were created as a result. Businesses that restrict and withhold information from employees smother their imagination. Measuring results is essential for imagination to work. We can't imagine a better way until we measure the results of what we are already doing. Without measurement we never know whether our better way really worked.

The internet, e-mail and social media may help or hurt people's imagination ability. On the one hand, ready access to a great variety of information should enhance imagination. On the other hand, imagination requires time to think, focus and analyze without distractions. In fact, we are most imaginative when we are bored. When bored our minds don't stay blank. We start thinking about how to serve the customer better and run the business better. Current internet, e-mail and social media is very distracting to businesspeople, and they need to control them not let them control the businessperson.

8-31 Innovation Processes

Q. How can I be more innovative in my business?

A. Innovation is a hot business topic right now second only to social media marketing. A recent survey of business CEOs indicated they thought innovation was 9 on a scale of 10 in importance for their business's success. However, the CEOs rated their own company's innovation less than 5 on a scale of 10. In my career I found chance was about 50 percent of business success. Ability, hard work and perseverance by managers and key employees was about 40 percent and innovation 10 percent. That said, innovation is important because it creates competitive advantages.

The innovation process is usually thought to consist of making analogies of existing innovative ideas to completely different situations, brainstorming possible off the wall solutions by a diverse team of collaborators, testing and evaluating potential solutions and finally choosing the solution most likely to succeed. The right process starts with a goal to improve a product, service, situation or business process. Then you break the goal into its components and use the following five step process.

First, subtract seemingly essential components from the product, service, situation, or process. Successful examples are subtracting eye glass frames to produce contact lens, back wheels of bicycles to produce exercise bikes and bank teller services to produce ATMs.

Second, combine tasks and functions to improve the product, service, situation, or process. A successful example is the backpack. Students and businesspeople use heavy backpacks to carry books, materials, and laptops. The backpack straps cut into the shoulders and are uncomfortable. One supplier widened and relocated the straps to press on the shiatsu nerve centers that convey a messaging affect.

Third, add components the product, service, situation, or process needs to improve its functioning and usefulness. One company added a second blade to its then new razor. The first blade is designed to pull the hair follicle away from the skin. The second blade is designed to cut the hair follicle close to the skin. Other examples are bifocal eyeglasses and double-sided tape.

Fourth, separate and rearrange the components of the product, service, situation, or process. Successful examples are enabling airline passengers to print their boarding pass on their personal computer and the TV remote that moved the controls from the TV monitor to any place in the room. Fifth, change the attributes of the product, service, situation, or process in response to a change in some other attribute. Examples are eyeglasses that change to become sunglasses in bright sunlight and a very old one of price discounts to repeat customers.

8-32 Learning from Business Competitors

Q. What can I learn from my competitors and about my competitors?

A. There are many areas where it's in the best interest of competitors to cooperate with each other. In some cases, by cooperating both competitors are able to increase their sales. One contractor or business may not have the employees, skills, experience, equipment, or credit to take on a project or large order themselves. They can either partner with a competitor or take the project or order as the general contractor and subcontract portions of the work with a competitor. Always have a written agreement stating each parties' duties and responsibilities.

It's in the common interest of competitors to ensure that customers receive the quality and service they expect. Otherwise, their unhappy experience will reflect on all competitors. That's the reason many industry trade associations set minimum standards for quality and service for their members. If a business doesn't have the product or service a customer needs or if they are too busy to serve the customer, they will refer the customer to a competitor. Competitors often share information about wage and salary rates either one on one or in area industry surveys. It's in their common interest to be competitive in compensation but not overpay or under pay.

Competitors often share best industry practices for producing their product or service to improve quality and service and reduce costs. That also may be done one on one or in industry surveys. Likewise, they share best practices for things like employee safety, environmental and other regulatory compliance. Competitors work with each other in lobbying public officials on business regulations and public relations.

There are also several sources to get information from or about competitors. In doing so don't misrepresent yourself or lie. Be up front with the sources. Common suppliers are likely to know what products and volumes your competitors buy and be willing to tell you. The supplier's motive is to satisfy all customers and sell as much as possible. Common customers may know a lot about your competitor's products and volumes as well as their quality, service, prices, product choices and convenience. A business that loses a project bid or large order to a competitor should always visit the customer and try to find out why they lost the business and why the competitor got the business. You can learn a lot about what that customer values most whether low price, best quality, good service, better choices, better convenience, or better reliability. Then you are prepared to compete better next time.

If a competitor's current or former employee applies for a job with your business, that's a good information source. Again, be honest and up front. Try to establish a business friendship with competitors. You'll be surprised how willing they will be to share information and help you.

8-33 Optimism and Pessimism in Business

Q. How can I be more optimistic and less pessimistic in my business?

A. Researchers in human behavior say to be more optimistic we need to learn to be more compassionate toward ourselves. Optimistic and self-compassionate people cope better with all sorts of problems in business and in life. Treat yourself as you would treat a good friend or relative. You wouldn't yell at a good friend or relative for minor failures-don't yell at yourself. Self-compassionate people cope with and compensate for their weaknesses. They don't have unrealistic expectations of themselves. They can accept and learn from failures and laugh at themselves.

Experts say we can learn self-compassion and optimism. Our outlook is influenced by genetics, experiences and how we interpret our experiences. We can't change genetics, but we can change our experiences and especially how we interpret our experiences. We all have optimistic and pessimistic circuits in our brains. The pessimistic circuit helps us identify threats and respond to avoid or mitigate the consequences. Our optimistic circuit is in the brain's pleasure center and focuses on the good things in life. People who are optimistic and cope well have a wide range of emotions from positive to negative. We need four good emotions to offset one bad emotion. Any less and our optimism and attitude toward life deteriorates.

Train yourself to look for and focus on the positive events that occur each day. One useful way to do that is to keep a journal and record the positive and negative events of each day. Record the things you're grateful for. Working on other's problems puts ours in better perspective. Christians believe that in helping others we help ourselves. We extend our boundaries and in being concerned about others we are less concerned about ourselves. Vent your frustrations to a friend and in turn let them vent their frustrations to you. Compare your problems to those less fortunate in life. That puts your problems in better perspective. Project yourself forward in time one to five years and ask yourself how important the present problem will be then. In most cases it won't matter.

With all the above said, there are times and situations in business when we need to be optimistic and others where we need to be pessimistic. Selling, motivating, leading and speaking require optimism. Planning and major decisions require a measured degree of pessimism to identify and evaluate the potential bad outcomes. Up business cycles call for optimism to take risks and seize the opportunities. Good timing often creates more business success than smartness and hard work. Down business cycles call for caution and the right amount of pessimism to prepare for hard times.

www.ingramcontent.com/pod-product-compliance
Lightning Source LLC
Chambersburg PA
CBHW020636220526
45464CB00001B/178